barbecue bible

224 delicious recipes

p

This is a Parragon Publishing Book
This edition published in 2006

Parragon Publishing
Queen Street House
4 Queen Street
Bath BA1 1HE
United Kingdom

This edition designed by Talking Design Ltd,
Worthing, West Sussex

ISBN: 1-40546-643-X

Printed in China

NOTE
Cup measurements in this book are for American cups. This book also uses imperial and metric
measurements. Follow the same units of measurement throughout; do not mix imperial and
metric. All spoon measurements are level: teaspoons are assumed to be 5 ml and tablespoons
are assumed to be 15 ml. Unless otherwise stated, milk is assumed to be whole milk, eggs and
individual vegetables such as potatoes are medium, and pepper is freshly ground black pepper.

The times given for each recipe are an approximate guide only because the preparation times may
differ according to the techniques used by different people and the cooking times may vary as a
result of the type of oven used.

Recipes using raw or very lightly cooked eggs should be avoided by infants, the elderly, pregnant
women, convalescents, and anyone suffering from an illness.

contents

why BBQ?

In short, fun, friends, and fine hearty food. Barbecuing is about delicious steaks or homemade burgers, fresh fish, and colorful vegetables, and the sizzle and hiss of cooking in the background, merging with the bubble of conversation.

Good barbecuing means that the ritual of cooking is almost as important as the food itself. It is the one time that you can excuse blackened food, and for once taste, rather than presentation, is the key.

A barbecue, when properly organized, can be one of the easiest, most sociable, and most flexible of food activities. A barbecue can start early in the afternoon and stretch lazily into the evening. The smell of someone else's barbecue on a warm summer evening is all the incentive you should need!

Basic barbecuing in ten easy steps

1. Choose your type of barbecue:
- Portable - light and easy to carry, ideal for a picnic if you are not walking too far.
- Disposable - made of a small foil tray with a wire rack and fuel supplied. They last up to an hour and can only be used once.
- Brazier - portable to a limited extent; some have legs and others have wheels, some also have a hood to protect the food.
- Gas - very popular as they are clean, quick and easy to use. Models with flavorizer bars will produce food with that tasty, smoky flavor.
- Kettle grill - with a hood, these are versatile and efficient. Some have a rotisserie attachment.
- Permanent/custom-built - can be built into your yard, in the right spot and do not have to be expensive.

2. Choose your fuel:
- Lumpwood charcoal - easy to ignite, but will burn quite quickly. Inexpensive and easily available.
- Charcoal briquettes - can take a while to light, but burn for a long period with little smoke and smell.
- Self-igniting charcoal - is lumpwood charcoal or charcoal briquettes coated with a flammable chemical. Easy to light. Wait until the chemical has burned off before adding food to the rack.
- Hardwoods - such as mesquite, oak, and apple give a pleasant aroma and burn slowly. Soft woods are not an appropriate fuel.

3. Get your gear sorted - remember grill gloves and tongs to turn things over!

4. Pick your spot - if you are not using a fixed barbecue then be sure to choose a spot that is stable and on a flat surface. Don't move the barbecue once it's lit.

5. Preparation - use kitchen foil to line the base of your barbecue underneath the fire grate. This will make cleaning easier and will keep the bottom of the barbecue hot.

6. Set up your fuel - spread a layer of fuel on to the fire grate: small pieces at the bottom and medium-sized pieces on top of them works best. The layer of charcoal or wood should be 2 inches deep and resemble a pyramid in the center of the grate (if you are using paraffin starters, see below).

7. Light the barbecue - if using paraffin starters, place one or two in the center of the pyramid. If using charcoal lighter fluid, pour a few tablespoons in the fuel and leave for a minute. Never use gasoline. Light the barbecue using a long match or taper and leave for 15 minutes. Remember to light your barbecue at least 1 hour before you want to start cooking.

8. Raising the temperature - spread the coals into an even layer and leave for 40 minutes, or until they are covered with a thin layer of gray ash and are hot enough to begin cooking. Spread the hot coals at least 1 inch farther than the area on which you will be cooking the food.

9. **Controlling the barbecue -** to control the heat of the barbecue for cooking, raise or lower the grill rack. If your barbecue has air vents, open these to raise the temperature of the barbecue and close them to lower it. You can also push the hot coals carefully into the center of the barbecue to provide a higher heat in the middle and a lower heat nearer the edges where you can put food once it is cooked.

10. **Cooking the food -** always make sure that food is thoroughly cooked through (see cooking times below). The barbecue needs to be very hot before you start cooking. Do not overcrowd food on the barbecue rack as individual pieces of food will not cook properly. Do not mix meat, vegetables, and fish on the same rack. When cooking meat, turn steaks and burgers once, turn kabobs and sausages frequently. Brush the rack with a little sunflower oil (but not too much) to stop meat sticking.

Your complete guide to the finest ingredients

Beef

Cooking times

- Steaks 1 inch thick should be cooked over hot coals for 8 minutes. Cook for 5 minutes if you prefer steak rare, and for 12 minutes if you prefer it well done.
- Burgers 3/4 inch thick should be cooked over hot coals for 6-8 minutes.
- Kabobs made with medium-sized pieces of beef should be cooked for 7 minutes over hot coals.

Cuts of beef for barbecuing

Only the best cuts are suitable for barbecuing as it requires little cooking and has a superb taste. The majority of beef recipes in this book use:

- Sirloin - the tenderest cut from the back of the loin. It can be a large joint on the bone for roasting, but also provides tasty steaks for barbecuing.
- Rib-eye (also known as Delmonico) steak - comes from the small end of the rib roast. It is thought to have the best flavor of all the steaks and can be cut into any size. Other cuts of beef include:
- Tenderloin or fillet steak - the finest cut of beef: it is lean and boneless. It comes from below the sirloin and is the most expensive.
- Strip steak - the top loin without the tenderloin. A very popular type of steak and very lean with a firm texture.
- T-bone - a steak from the thin end of the short loin containing a T-shaped bone and piece of tenderloin.

Choosing red meat

Red meats should look fresh and moist but not too red. If the meat is bright red, it will not have hung enough to develop a good flavor. A ruby/burgundy color is better. The fat should be creamy rather than white. Trim fat from meat as excess fat dripping onto the coals could ignite.

Lamb
Cooking times

- Leg steaks should be cooked over medium hot coals for 10-15 minutes. If they are thicker than 3/4 inch, increase the cooking time or use a meat mallet to tenderize and flatten them a little.
- Chops 1 inch thick are best cooked over medium hot coals for 15 minutes.
- Kabobs made with 1 inch cubes of lamb should be cooked for about 8-15 minutes over medium hot coals.

Cuts of lamb for barbecuing

Recipes in this book include;

- Leg steaks - more of a slice of meat than a chop and with a central bone.
- Rack of lamb - a very small joint, but very tender. It is easy to carve by cutting down between the bones.
- Loin chops - cut from the loin and have a T-shaped bone.
- Fillet - a boneless strip of meat, cut from the middle neck. It is good cut into cubes and made into kabobs for the barbecue.
- Shoulder of lamb - has a sweet flavor.
- Leg of lamb - is a tender and lean joint.

Another cut of lamb is:

- Cutlets - very small chops, cut from the tips of the ribs, with tender sweet meat and long, thin bones. Serve 2-3 per person.

Pork
Cooking times

- Cook chops for 15-20 minutes over medium hot coals and make sure that they are cooked through. If they are thicker than 1 inch, increase the cooking time accordingly.
- Kabobs made with 1 inch cubes of pork should be cooked for about 15 minutes over medium hot coals.
- Most pork spare ribs are quite thick and will need to be cooked over medium hot coals for 40 minutes to make sure that they are cooked thoroughly.
- Thick sausages will need 10 minutes over medium hot coals; thinner ones may be ready slightly earlier.

Cuts of pork for barbecuing

Recipes in this book include:

- Spare ribs - cut from the thick end of belly pork.
- Tenderloin - is a very lean cut with no waste. It can also be cut into cubes and made into kabobs or just cut into rounds as medallions.
- Chops - most recipes don't specify types of chops to be used, but loin chops are large lean chops, cut from the center of the animal, with a good edge of fat that needs to be trimmed before barbecuing.

Choosing pork

Pork flesh should be smooth and moist and a pale pink color. Organic pork will have a higher percentage of fat than factory-farmed pork (make sure this is trimmed before barbecuing) and will certainly have a better flavor. Sausages should contain at least 80% meat.

Chicken

Cooking times

- Quarters, legs, and breasts with a bone should be cooked for 35 minutes over medium hot coals.
- Cook chicken drumsticks for 25-35 minutes over medium hot coals until the juices run clear, not pink, when you pierce the thickest part of the leg with a skewer or the point of a knife. If the drumsticks are very large, increase the cooking time.
- Whole breasts will need to be cooked over medium to hot coals for 15-20 minutes.
- Kabobs made with 1 inch cubes of chicken should be cooked through after 10 minutes over medium hot coals.

Cuts of chicken for barbecuing

All chicken is suitable for barbecuing. The breasts are best if left on the bone because they will stay moister. It is a good idea to marinate chicken pieces before cooking, because this helps the meat stay moist while cooking.

Choosing chicken

Always try to use fresh chicken for barbecuing. Choose fresh birds that look soft, plump, and creamy pink; they should not be scrawny, discolored or bruised.

Fish & Seafood

Cooking times

- Cook whole small fish, up to 900g/2lb over medium hot coals for 5-7 minutes.
- Fish steaks, such as salmon or tuna, or fish fillets up to 1 inch thick, should be cooked for 6-10 minutes over medium hot coals.
- Fish kabobs made with 1 inch cubes of fish should be cooked over medium hot coals for 7 minutes.
- Shrimp in their shells should be cooked over medium hot coals for 7 minutes if they are large. Smaller shrimp should be threaded onto kabob skewers. Large peeled shrimp will cook slightly faster.

Choosing Fish & Seafood

- If a fish or seafood has a "fishy odor" the product is already in decline and consequently will not taste pleasant.
- Gills should be deep red in color, clean and clear of any mucus. Gills that are brown in color suggest a lack of freshness.

- Raw shrimp should be moist, firm, and smell of the sea. Do not buy shrimp that have either an ammonia smell or a fishy smell.
- Ask someone on the fish counter to gut whole fish, or take the head and tail off, if you wish.

Vegetables & Salads

Vegetables

You can barbecue nearly any vegetable. The best vegetables for barbecuing are eggplant, mushrooms, zucchini, bell peppers, and corncobs. If you are cooking from raw, some vegetables do take a while to cook. There are individual recipes in this cookbook, but as a general rule you can speed up the process by parboiling vegetables indoors until they are nearly done.

Barbecue as follows:
- Brush with oil and sprinkle them with seasonings.
- Cook over medium hot coals. You can thread a variety of vegetables on skewers to make them easier to manage, or you can cut large vegetables in half and barbecue them individually.
- Turn the vegetables frequently, as they burn easily.

Salads

Of course, no barbecue would be complete without a deliciously crisp side salad. Fresh ingredients are the key to a fantastic salad and remember, if it is a hot day, don't leave your salad outside while you are cooking, keep it cool indoors until it is time to serve.

Choosing and preparing salad leaves
- When choosing salad greens look for firm leaves of good color with no signs of browning or slime.
- They should be used within about two days of purchase, although very crisp lettuces, such as iceberg and romaine can be stored in the salad drawer of the refrigerator for up to five days.
- Bags of mixed leaves are treated with oxygen to prolong their shelf life, but once the bag has been opened, they deteriorate very rapidly.
- To prepare, discard any coarse or wilted outer leaves and carefully wash the remainder in cold water. Drain well and then dry in a salad spinner or by wrapping them in a clean dish towel, as oil-based dressings will not adhere to wet leaves.

chargrilledburgerssteaksmmmmflavor
glowingcoals...

beef

steak with parsley butter

SERVES	PREP	COOK
2	**5** mins	**2-8** mins

The savory herb butter in this recipe can be prepared well in advance and frozen, then used straight from the freezer, which makes this a very quick meal to prepare.

1 To make the parsley butter, put the butter into a bowl and beat until smooth, then beat in the parsley, lemon juice, salt and cayenne pepper. Spoon onto a sheet of baking parchment and roll into a log. Wrap the parchment around it and twist the ends. The roll should be about 1 inch/2.5 cm thick. Chill in the refrigerator for 2 hours, or until firm, or freeze for future use.

2 Preheat the barbecue. Brush the steaks with the melted butter and a little oil and season with salt and pepper. Cook the steaks over hot coals for 2–4 minutes on each side for rare to medium.

3 Unwrap the parsley butter and cut into slices. Cut the parsley butter into several slices and top each steak with 2 slices. Serve at once.

Ingredients

- 2 tbsp butter, melted
- 1 tbsp sunflower-seed oil
- 2 sirloin or rib-eye steaks, about 8 oz/175 g each and 1 inch/2.5 cm thick, at room temperature
- salt and pepper

for the parsley butter
- ½ stick unsalted butter, softened
- 1½ tbsp very finely chopped fresh flat-leaf parsley
- squeeze of lemon juice
- cayenne pepper

thai-spiced beef & bell pepper kabobs

SERVES **4**

PREP **20** **mins**

+2½ hrs marinating

COOK **10-15** **mins**

This dish offers a spicy, flavorsome treat for a special barbecue party.

1 Put the sherry, rice wine, soy sauce, hoisin sauce, garlic, chili, ginger, and scallions into a large bowl and mix until well combined. Season to taste.

2 Thread the meat onto 8 skewers, alternating it with chunks of red bell pepper. When the skewers are full (leave a small space at either end), transfer them to the bowl and turn them in the soy sauce mixture until they are well coated. Cover with plastic wrap and place in the refrigerator to marinate for 2½ hours or overnight.

3 When the skewers are thoroughly marinated, lift them out and grill them over hot coals, turning them frequently, for 10–15 minutes or until the meat is cooked right through. Serve at once on a bed of green and red lettuce.

ingredients

marinade
2 tbsp sherry
2 tbsp rice wine
scant ⅓ cup soy sauce
scant ⅓ cup hoisin sauce
3 cloves garlic, finely chopped
1 red chili, seeded and
  finely chopped
1½ tbsp grated fresh gingerroot
3 scallions, trimmed and finely
  chopped
salt and pepper

kabobs
2 lb 4 oz/1 kg loin end or short
  loin steak, cubed
2 large red bell peppers, seeded
  and cut into small chunks

to serve
green and red lettuce

italian steak melt burgers

SERVES	PREP	+30	COOK
4	**20** mins	**mins** chilling	**8-13** mins

Ring the changes and use mozzarella cheese, fontina, Bel Paese, or even Gorgonzola in this recipe. These delicious burgers are ideal served as part of a barbecue party or an informal supper dish.

1 Place the ground steak, onion, garlic, red bell pepper, olives, pepper and tomato paste in a food processor and, using the pulse button, blend together. Shape into 4 equal-size burgers, then cover and let chill for at least 30 minutes.

2 Preheat the barbecue. Place the burgers on the rack and cook, turning carefully for 6 – 8 minutes, or until cooked to personal preference.

3 Place a tomato slice on top of each burger, then place the cheese over the tomato. Cook for an additional 2–3 minutes, or until the cheese starts to melt. Serve.

ingredients

1 lb/450 g best ground steak
1 onion, grated
2–4 garlic cloves, crushed
1 small red bell pepper, seeded, peeled, and chopped
$1/3$ cup pitted black olives, finely chopped
pepper
1 tbsp tomato paste
2 large tomatoes, thickly sliced
3 oz/85 g Gruyère cheese, sliced

beef teriyaki

SERVES	PREP		COOK
4	**10** mins	**+2hrs** marinating	**10-20** mins

This Japanese-style teriyaki sauce complements beef, but it can also be used to accompany chicken or salmon.

1 Place the beef steaks in a shallow, nonmetallic dish. To make the sauce, mix the cornstarch and sherry together in a small bowl, then stir in the remaining sauce ingredients. Pour the sauce over the meat, cover with plastic wrap, and let marinate in the refrigerator for at least 2 hours.

2 Preheat the barbecue. Remove the meat from the sauce and reserve. Pour the sauce into a small pan and heat gently until it is just simmering, stirring occasionally.

3 Cut the meat into thin strips and thread these, concertina-style, on to several presoaked wooden skewers, alternating each strip of meat with the pieces of bell pepper and scallion. Cook the kabobs over hot coals for 5–8 minutes, turning and basting the beef and vegetables occasionally with the reserved sauce.

4 Arrange the skewers on serving plates, pour over the remaining sauce, and serve with salad greens.

ingredients

1 lb/450 g extra thin beef steaks
1 yellow bell pepper, seeded and
  cut into chunks
8 scallions, trimmed and cut into
  short lengths

sauce
1 tsp cornstarch
2 tbsp dry sherry
2 tbsp white wine vinegar
3 tbsp soy sauce
1 tbsp dark brown sugar
1 garlic clove, crushed
$^1/_2$ tsp ground cinnamon
$^1/_2$ tsp ground ginger

to serve
salad greens

ingredients

1 small onion, finely chopped
1 tbsp chopped fresh cilantro
large pinch of paprika
$1/4$ tsp allspice
$1/4$ tsp ground coriander
$1/4$ tsp brown sugar
1 lb/450 g ground beef
salt and pepper
vegetable oil, for brushing

to garnish
fresh cilantro leaves

to serve
freshly cooked bulgur wheat
  or rice
mixed salad

greek-style beef kabobs

SERVES	PREP	COOK
4	**25** mins	**15-20** mins

Your barbecue party can take on a Greek theme with these tasty kabobs.

1 Put the onion, fresh cilantro, spices, sugar, and beef into a large bowl and mix until well combined.

2 On a clean counter, use your hands to shape the mixture into sausages around skewers. Brush them lightly with vegetable oil.

3 Grill the kabobs over hot coals, turning them frequently, for 15–20 minutes or until cooked right through. Arrange the kabobs on a platter of freshly cooked bulgur wheat or rice and garnish with fresh cilantro leaves. Serve with a mixed salad.

ingredients

2 lb 4 oz/1 kg lean steak,
  ground
1 cup fresh bread crumbs
1 egg, lightly beaten
1 tbsp chopped fresh thyme
salt and pepper

to serve
6 burger buns
lettuce leaves
red onion slices
tomato slices
dill pickle slices (optional)
tomato ketchup, relishes,
  mustard of choice

classic burger in a bun

SERVES
6

PREP
5
mins

+30
mins
chilling

COOK
6-10
mins

This is a terrific meal for children—irresistible homemade burgers they can assemble themselves.

1 Put the ground steak, bread crumbs, egg, and thyme in a bowl and season with salt and pepper. Mix thoroughly, using your hands.

2 Divide the mixture into 6 portions and shape each into a circle. Place on a plate, cover, and let chill for 30 minutes to firm up.

3 Cook the burgers over a medium barbecue for 3–5 minutes on each side, depending on how well done you like them. Turn them carefully as they will not be as firm as store-bought burgers. Split the burger buns and toast them, cut-side down, until golden. Place a burger in each bun and serve with a selection of fillings and accompaniments (well away from the barbecue fire).

mustard steaks

SERVES
4

PREP
10
mins

+1hr
cooling/
standing

COOK
50-60
mins

Tarragon mustard gives these steaks a subtle spicy flavor that contrasts well with the sharp taste of the sweet-and-sour tomato relish.

1 To make the tomato relish, place all the ingredients in a heavy-bottomed pan, seasoning to taste with salt. Bring to a boil, stirring, until the sugar has completely dissolved. Lower the heat and simmer, stirring occasionally, for 40 minutes, or until thickened. Transfer to a bowl, cover with plastic wrap, and let cool.

2 Preheat the barbecue. Using a sharp knife, cut almost completely through each steak horizontally to make a pocket. Spread the mustard inside the pockets and rub the steaks all over with the garlic. Place the steaks on a plate, cover with plastic wrap, and let stand for 30 minutes.

3 Cook the steaks over hot coals for 2$\frac{1}{2}$ minutes each side for rare, 4 minutes each side for medium, or 6 minutes each side for well done. Transfer to serving plates, garnish with fresh tarragon sprigs, and serve immediately with the tomato relish.

ingredients

4 sirloin or rump steaks
1 tbsp tarragon mustard
2 garlic cloves, crushed

tomato relish
8 oz/225 g cherry tomatoes
2 oz/55 g raw brown sugar
2 fl oz/50 ml white wine vinegar
1 piece of preserved ginger, chopped
$\frac{1}{2}$ lime, thinly sliced
salt

to garnish
sprigs of fresh tarragon

indonesian beef kabobs

SERVES	PREP		COOK
4	**15** mins	**+2hrs** marinating/ standing	**10** mins

These spicy Indonesian kabobs are traditionally served with sambal kecap—a delicious chili-flavored dipping sauce—and a refreshing cucumber salad.

1 To make the sauce, using a sharp knife, deseed the chili and finely chop. Place in a small bowl with all the other sauce ingredients and mix together. Cover with plastic wrap and let stand until required.

2 Dry-fry the coriander and cumin seeds in a skillet for 1 minute, or until they give off their aroma and start to pop. Remove from the heat and grind in a mortar with a pestle. Place the steak in a shallow, nonmetallic dish and add the ground spices, stirring to coat. Put the onion, garlic, sugar, soy sauce, and lemon juice into a food processor and process to a paste. Season to taste with salt and spoon the mixture over the steak, turning to coat. Cover with plastic wrap and let marinate in the refrigerator for 2 hours.

3 Preheat the barbecue. Drain the steak, reserving the marinade, and thread it onto several presoaked wooden or metal skewers. Cook over hot coals, turning and basting frequently with the reserved marinade, for 5–8 minutes, until thoroughly cooked. Transfer to a large serving plate and serve with the sauce for dipping.

ingredients

1 tsp coriander seeds
1/2 tsp cumin seeds
1 lb/450 g rump steak, cut into strips
1 onion
2 garlic cloves
1 tbsp brown sugar
1 tbsp dark soy sauce
1 tbsp lemon juice

rump steak with dark barbecue sauce

SERVES
6

PREP
10
mins

+4hrs
marinating

COOK
30-35
mins

This barbecue favorite is marinated in a spicy sauce and served with a topping of shallot butter.

1 Heat the oil in a large skillet. Cook the onion over low heat, stirring occasionally, for 5 minutes, or until softened. Stir in the tomatoes, lemon juice, Tabasco and Worcestershire sauces, sugar, and mustard powder. Cover and let simmer, stirring occasionally, for 15–20 minutes, or until thickened. Pour into a large dish and let cool.

2 Meanwhile, blanch the shallots in boiling water for 2–3 minutes. Drain well and pat dry with paper towels. Place in a food processor and process to a purée. Gradually work in the butter and season with salt and pepper. Scrape the shallot butter into a bowl, cover, and let chill until required.

3 Add the steaks to the cooled marinade, turning to coat. Cover and let marinate in a cool place for 4 hours.

4 Drain the steaks, reserving the marinade. Grill on a hot barbecue, brushing frequently with the marinade, for 2 minutes on each side for rare, 4 minutes on each side for medium, or 6 minutes on each side for well done. Serve each steak topped with a spoonful of shallot butter and garnish with watercress sprigs.

ingredients

2 tbsp corn oil

marinade
1 onion, finely chopped
1 lb/450 g tomatoes, peeled,
  seeded, and chopped
2 tbsp lemon juice
1 tbsp Tabasco sauce
2 tbsp Worcestershire sauce
2 tbsp brown sugar
1 tsp mustard powder

5 oz/140 g shallots,
  finely chopped
5 oz/140 g butter, softened
6 rump steaks, about 6 oz/
  175 g each
salt and pepper

to garnish
few sprigs of watercress

new orleans steak sandwich

SERVES
4

PREP
10-12
mins

COOK
30-35
mins

An aristocratic relation of the humble burger, this is a positive feast for serious meateaters.

1 Heat half the oil in a heavy-bottom skillet. Add the onions and garlic, sprinkle with a pinch of salt, then cover and cook over very low heat for 25–30 minutes, or until very soft and caramelized.

2 Process the onion mixture in a food processor until smooth. Scrape into a bowl, stir in the vinegar, thyme, parsley, and mustard and season with salt and pepper. Cover and place at the side of the barbecue.

3 Brush the steaks with the remaining oil and season with salt and pepper. Grill on a hot barbecue for 2 minutes on each side for rare, 4 minutes on each side for medium, or 6 minutes on each side for well done.

4 Meanwhile, toast the bread on both sides. Spread the onion mixture on the toast. Slice the steaks and top 4 toast slices with the meat. Sprinkle with the crumbled Roquefort, then add the tomatoes and lettuce leaves. Top with the remaining toast and serve.

ingredients

4 tbsp olive oil
2 large onions, sliced thinly
into rings
2 garlic cloves, chopped
1 tbsp red wine vinegar
1 tbsp chopped fresh thyme
3 tbsp chopped fresh parsley
2 tsp prepared mild mustard

beef satay

SERVES	PREP		COOK
6	**10** mins	**+2hrs** marinating	**5-8** mins

Many Westerners assume that a satay must involve a peanut sauce, but this is not always true. The term simply refers to a kabob that has been marinated in a flavorsome mixture of any kind.

1 Using a sharp knife, cut the steak into 1-inch/2.5-cm cubes, then place in a large, shallow, nonmetallic dish. Mix the honey, soy sauce, oil, garlic, coriander, caraway seeds, and chili powder together in a small measuring cup. Pour the mixture over the steak and stir until the steak is thoroughly coated with the marinade. Cover with plastic wrap and let marinate in the refrigerator for 2 hours, turning occasionally.

2 Preheat the barbecue. Drain the steak, reserving the marinade. Thread the steak onto several presoaked wooden skewers.

3 Cook the steak over hot coals, turning and brushing frequently with the reserved marinade, for 5–8 minutes. Transfer to a large serving plate, garnish with lime wedges, and serve.

ingredients

2 lb 4 oz/1 kg rump steak
1 tbsp honey
2 tbsp dark soy sauce
2 tbsp peanut oil
1 garlic clove, finely chopped
1 tsp ground coriander
1 tsp caraway seeds
pinch of chili powder

to garnish
lime wedges

beefburgers with chili and basil

SERVES **4**   **PREP** **10** mins   **COOK** **10-16** mins

A tasty traditional barbecue dish—with an extra spiciness.

1 Put the ground beef, red bell pepper, garlic, chilies, chopped basil, and cumin into a bowl and mix until well combined. Season with salt and pepper.

2 Using your hands, form the mixture into burger shapes. Barbecue the burgers over hot coals for 5–8 minutes on each side, or until cooked right through. Garnish with sprigs of basil and serve in hamburger buns.

ingredients

1 lb 7 oz/650 g ground beef
1 red bell pepper, seeded and
  finely chopped
1 garlic clove, finely chopped
2 small red chilies, seeded and
  finely chopped
1 tbsp chopped fresh basil
1/2 tsp ground cumin
salt and pepper

to garnish
sprigs of fresh basil

to serve
hamburger buns

middle eastern koftas

SERVES 4

PREP 10 mins

COOK 10 mins

For a twist to the normal barbecue kabob try these koftas which are quick and easy to make and taste delicious.

1 Process the meat, onion, garlic, parsley, spices, and seasoning to a smooth paste in a food processor. Turn into a large mixing bowl.

2 Select flat skewers that fit comfortably onto your barbecue rack.

3 Take about 2 tablespoons of meat paste and roll gently between your palms to make a sausage shape. Carefully fold around the skewer. If you cannot find flat skewers, shape the meat into patties as you would for hamburgers.

4 Preheat the barbecue. Brush the koftas with minted yogurt marinade and cook for 10 minutes over hot coals, turning carefully and basting regularly.

5 When the meat is cooked, transfer to a large serving platter and garnish with sprigs of fresh mint and lemon wedges. Serve with rice or Indian bread and bowls of cucumber yogurt raita and tomato onion salad.

ingredients

1 lb 10 oz/750 g ground
  lamb or beef
1 small onion, quartered
2 garlic cloves, crushed
2 tbsp chopped fresh
  flat leaf parsley
1 tsp coriander seeds
$1/2$ tsp cumin seeds
$1/2$ tsp whole black peppercorns
generous pinch of ground
  cinnamon
pinch of salt
Minted Yogurt Marinade
  (see page 218)

to garnish
fresh mint and lemon wedges

serving suggestions
rice or Indian bread
cucumber yogurt raita
tomato and onion salad

cheese and apple burgers

SERVES	PREP	+30	COOK
4-6	**10-12** mins	**mins** chilling	**12-18** mins

Savory cheese and sweet apple always seem to bring out the best in each other. Here they work their magic in a burger, adding melting texture and sharp flavor to the tender beef.

1 Place the ground steak in a large bowl. Add the onion, mustard, pepper, Worcestershire sauce to taste, and the grated cheese. Peel and core 1 of the apples, then grate and add to the bowl. Mix together, then shape into 4 equal-size burgers. Cover and let chill for 30 minutes.

2 Preheat the barbecue. Peel and core the remaining apple whole, then cut into 4–6 thick slices. Brush with melted butter and sprinkle with the superfine sugar. Place on a barbecue rack and cook for 2–3 minutes on each side or until caramelized. Set aside.

3 Cook the burgers over hot coals for 4–6 minutes on each side or until cooked to personal preference. Top the burgers with the sliced cheese and broil until the cheese has melted. Serve.

ingredients

1 lb/450 g best ground steak

1 onion, finely chopped

1–2 tsp whole-grain mustard, or to taste

pepper

2–3 tsp Worcestershire sauce

2 oz/55 g sharp Cheddar cheese, grated

2 Bramley apples

1 tbsp butter, melted

2–3 tsp superfine sugar

2 oz/55 g Gruyère cheese, thinly sliced

chopsizzlesausageribssensationalsauces
meatballstasty...

pork

sausages with barbecue sauce

SERVES	PREP	COOK
4	**5-8** mins	**30-35** mins

Although there is much more to barbecues than sausages, they can make a welcome appearance from time to time. This delicious sauce is a wonderful excuse for including them again.

1 To make the sauce, heat the oil in a small pan and sauté the onion and garlic for 4–5 minutes, until softened and just beginning to brown.

2 Add the tomatoes, Worcestershire sauce, brown fruity sauce, sugar, wine vinegar, chili powder, mustard powder, Tabasco sauce, and salt and pepper to taste and bring to a boil.

3 Reduce the heat and simmer gently for 10–15 minutes, until the sauce begins to thicken slightly. Stir occasionally so that the sauce does not burn and stick to the bottom of the pan. Set the sauce aside and keep warm until required.

4 Broil the sausages over hot coals for 10–15 minutes, turning frequently. Do not prick them with a fork or the juices and fat will run out and cause the barbecue to flare.

5 Put the sausages in the hot dog buns and serve with the barbecue sauce.

ingredients

2 tbsp sunflower oil
1 large onion, chopped
2 cloves garlic, chopped
8 ounce canned chopped
  tomatoes
1 tbsp Worcestershire sauce
2 tbsp brown fruity sauce
2 tbsp light muscovado sugar
4 tbsp white wine vinegar
$1/2$ tsp mild chili powder
$1/4$ tsp mustard powder
dash of Tabasco sauce
1 pound sausages
salt and pepper

to serve
hot dog buns

chinese ribs

Leave these pork spareribs to marinate for as long as possible to ensure that the wonderful flavors of the marinade mingle and thoroughly permeate the meat.

1 Place the spareribs in a large, shallow, nonmetallic dish. Mix the soy sauce, sugar, oil, garlic, Chinese five-spice powder, and ginger together in a measuring cup. Pour the mixture over the ribs and turn until the ribs are well coated in the marinade.

2 Cover the dish with plastic wrap and let marinate in the refrigerator for at least 6 hours.

3 Preheat the barbecue. Drain the ribs, reserving the marinade. Cook over medium hot coals, turning and brushing frequently with the reserved marinade, for 30–40 minutes. Transfer to a large serving dish, garnish with the shredded scallions, and serve immediately.

ingredients

2 lb 4 oz/1 kg pork spareribs, separated
4 tbsp dark soy sauce
3 tbsp brown sugar
1 tbsp peanut or sunflower-seed oil
2 garlic cloves, finely chopped
2 tsp Chinese five-spice powder
$^{1}/_{2}$-inch/1-cm piece fresh gingerroot, grated

to garnish
shredded scallions

pork burgers with tangy orange marinade

SERVES	PREP		COOK
4-6	**12** mins	**+1hr** marinating/chilling	**26-30** mins

The piquant flavor of orange juice and rind is the making of this burger. Even the large pieces of orange peel in the marmalade play their part by adding extra texture.

1 Place the pork in a shallow dish. Place the marmalade, orange juice, and vinegar in a small pan and heat, stirring, until the marmalade has melted. Pour the marinade over the pork. Cover and let stand for at least 30 minutes, or longer if time permits. Remove the pork, reserving the marinade. Grind the pork into a large bowl.

2 Meanwhile, cook the parsnips in a pan of boiling water for 15–20 minutes, or until cooked. Drain, then mash and add to the pork. Stir in the orange rind, garlic, scallions, zucchini, and salt and pepper to taste. Mix together, then shape into 4–6 equal-size burgers. Cover and let chill for at least 30 minutes.

3 Preheat the barbecue. When hot, add the burgers and cook over hot coals for 4–6 minutes on each side or until thoroughly cooked. Boil the reserved marinade for 3 minutes, then pour into a small pitcher or bowl. Serve.

ingredients

1 lb/450 g pork fillet, cut into small pieces
3 tbsp Seville orange marmalade
2 tbsp orange juice
1 tbsp balsamic vinegar
8 oz/225 g parsnips, cut into chunks
1 tbsp finely grated orange rind
2 garlic cloves, crushed
6 scallions, finely chopped
1 zucchini (6 oz/175 g), grated
salt and pepper
1 tbsp corn oil

normandy brochettes

SERVES **4** **PREP** **10** mins **+1-2 hrs** marinating **COOK** **12-15** mins

The orchards of Normandy are famous throughout France, providing both eating apples and cider-making varieties. For an authentic touch, enjoy a glass of Calvados between courses.

ingredients

1 lb/450 g pork fillet
1¼ cups hard cider
1 tbsp finely chopped fresh sage
6 black peppercorns, crushed
2 crisp eating apples
1 tbsp corn oil

1 Using a sharp knife, cut the pork into 1-inch/2.5-cm cubes, then place in a large, shallow, nonmetallic dish. Mix the cider, sage, and peppercorns together in a measuring cup, pour the mixture over the pork and turn until thoroughly coated. Cover and let marinate in the refrigerator for 1–2 hours.

2 Preheat the barbecue. Drain the pork, reserving the marinade. Core the apples, but do not peel, then cut into wedges. Dip the apple wedges into the reserved marinade and thread onto several metal skewers, alternating with the cubes of pork. Stir the corn oil into the remaining marinade.

3 Cook the brochettes over medium hot coals, turning and brushing frequently with the reserved marinade, for 12–15 minutes. Transfer to a large serving plate and if you prefer, remove the meat and apples from the skewers before serving. Serve immediately.

hot & spicy ribs

ingredients

1 onion, chopped
2 garlic cloves, chopped
1-inch/2.5-cm piece fresh
  gingerroot, sliced
1 fresh red chili, seeded
  and chopped
5 tbsp dark soy sauce
3 tbsp lime juice
1 tbsp jaggery or brown sugar
2 tbsp peanut oil
salt and pepper
2 lb 4 oz/1 kg pork spareribs,
  separated

SERVES	PREP	COOK
4	15 mins	1 hr

Twice-cooked (first in the kitchen and then on the barbecue), these succulent, pork spareribs are deliciously tender and packed full of spicy flavors.

1 Preheat the barbecue. Put the onion, garlic, ginger, chili, and soy sauce into a food processor and process to a paste. Transfer to a measuring cup and stir in the lime juice, sugar, and oil. Season with salt and pepper.

2 Place the spareribs in a preheated wok or large, heavy-bottom pan and pour in the soy sauce mixture. Place on the stove and bring to a boil, then let simmer over low heat, stirring frequently, for 30 minutes. If the mixture appears to be drying out, add a little water.

3 Remove the spareribs, reserving the sauce. Cook the ribs over medium hot coals, turning and basting frequently with the sauce, for 20–30 minutes. Transfer to a large serving plate and serve immediately.

grilled pork sausages with thyme

SERVES	PREP		COOK
4	**15** mins	**+45 mins** chilling	**15** mins

These sausages will make you rediscover the variety and joy of one of the best-loved barbecue foods.

1 Put the garlic, onion, chili, pork, almonds, bread crumbs, and fresh thyme into a large bowl. Season well with salt and pepper and mix until well combined.

2 Using your hands, form the mixture into sausage shapes. Roll each sausage in a little flour, then transfer to a bowl, cover with plastic wrap, and refrigerate for 45 minutes.

3 Brush a piece of aluminum foil with oil, then put the sausages on the foil and brush them with a little more vegetable oil. Transfer the sausages and foil to the barbecue grill. Grill over hot coals, turning the sausages frequently, for about 15 minutes or until cooked right through. Serve with bread rolls, cooked sliced onion, and tomato catsup and/or mustard.

ingredients

1 garlic clove, finely chopped
1 onion, grated
1 small red chili, seeded and
  finely chopped
1 lb/450 g lean ground pork
$^1/_3$ cup almonds, toasted
  and ground
1 cup fresh bread crumbs
1 tbsp finely chopped fresh thyme
salt and pepper
flour, for dusting
vegetable oil, for brushing

to serve
fresh bread rolls
slices of onion, lightly cooked
tomato catsup and/or mustard

pork & sage kabobs

MAKES
12

PREP
10-15
mins

+30
mins
chilling

COOK
8-10
mins

The ground pork mixture is shaped into meatballs and threaded onto skewers. They have a delicious, slightly sweet flavor that is popular with children.

1 Place the pork in a mixing bowl, together with the breadcrumbs, onion, sage, apple sauce, nutmeg, and salt and pepper to taste. Mix until the ingredients are well combined.

2 Using your hands, shape the mixture into small balls, about the size of large marbles, and chill in the refrigerator for at least 30 minutes.

3 Meanwhile, soak 12 small wooden skewers in cold water for at least 30 minutes. Thread the meatballs onto the skewers.

4 To make the baste, mix together the oil and lemon juice in a small bowl, whisking with a fork until it is well blended.

5 Broil the kabobs over hot coals for 8–10 minutes, turning and basting frequently with the lemon and oil mixture, until the meat is golden and cooked through.

6 Line the pita breads with the salad greens and spoon some of the yogurt on top. Serve with the kabobs.

ingredients

1 pound ground pork
$1/2$ cup fresh breadcrumbs
1 small onion, very finely chopped
1 tbsp fresh sage, chopped
2 tbsp apple sauce
$1/4$ tsp ground nutmeg
salt and pepper

baste
3 tbsp olive oil
1 tbsp lemon juice

to serve
6 small pita breads
mixed salad greens
6 tbsp thick, unsweetened yogurt

meatballs on sticks

SERVES	PREP	COOK
8	**20** mins	**10** mins

ingredients

4 pork and herb sausages
$1/2$ cup fresh ground beef
$1^1/2$ cups fresh white bread
  crumbs
1 onion, finely chopped
2 tbsp chopped mixed fresh
  herbs, such as parsley, thyme,
  and sage
1 egg
salt and pepper
corn oil, for brushing

to serve
sauces of your choice

These are popular with children and adults alike. Serve with a selection of ready-made or homemade sauces.

1 Preheat the barbecue. Remove the sausage meat from the skins, place in a large bowl and break up with a fork. Add the ground beef, bread crumbs, onion, herbs, and egg. Season to taste with salt and pepper and stir well with a wooden spoon until thoroughly mixed.

2 Form the mixture into small balls, about the size of a golf ball, between the palms of your hands. Spear each one with a toothpick and brush with oil.

3 Cook over medium hot coals, turning frequently and brushing with more oil as necessary, for 10 minutes, or until cooked through. Transfer to a large serving plate and serve immediately with a choice of sauces.

pork medallions with grilled apples

SERVES	PREP	+8-12	COOK
4	15-20 mins	hrs marinating	40-45 mins

This tasty chargrilled treat needs to be served with no more than a mixed salad and some crusty bread.

1 Make the marinade. Heat the oil and cook the garlic and shallots over low heat, stirring occasionally, for 5 minutes, until soft. Stir in the remaining marinade ingredients and let simmer gently for 5 minutes. Remove from the heat and let cool completely.

2 Cut the pork fillet into medallions about 1/2 inch/1 cm thick and place in a shallow dish. Pour in the marinade, turning to coat. Cover with plastic wrap and let marinate in the refrigerator overnight.

3 With a sharp knife, score through the skin of each apple around the center. Place each apple on a square of foil and put a rosemary sprig and 1 tsp sugar in each cavity. Enclose the apples in the foil and cook on a medium barbecue, turning occasionally, for 25–30 minutes.

4 About 10–15 minutes before the apples are ready, drain the pork, reserving the marinade. Grill, brushing with the reserved marinade for about 5 minutes on each side. Put 3–4 medallions on each plate with an unwrapped apple. Garnish with extra rosemary sprigs and serve.

ingredients

1 lb 2 oz/500 g pork fillet
4 eating apples, cored
4 small rosemary sprigs, plus
   extra to garnish
4 tsp superfine sugar

marinade

2 tbsp olive oil
1 garlic clove, finely chopped
4 shallots, finely chopped
4 tbsp orange juice
2 tbsp honey
1 tbsp Worcestershire sauce
1 tsp Dijon mustard
3 tbsp white wine vinegar
1 rosemary sprig, finely
   chopped

pigs in blankets

SERVES	PREP	COOK
4	15 mins	15-20 mins

Sausages are traditional fare for the barbecue, but even speciality varieties can a be a little boring. Pigs in blankets, on the other hand, are always delicious and fun.

ingredients

4 oz/115 g mozzarella cheese
8 Polish sausage links
2 tbsp Dijon mustard
8 smoked bacon strips

1 Preheat the barbecue. Thinly slice the mozzarella cheese. Cut a deep slit in the side of each sausage, using a sharp knife. Spread the cut sides with the mustard. Divide the slices of cheese between the sausages and reshape them.

2 Stretch the bacon with a heavy, flat-bladed knife. Wrap 1 bacon strip tightly round each sausage to hold it together. If necessary, secure with a toothpick.

3 Cook over hot coals, turning frequently, for 15–20 minutes. Transfer to a large serving plate and serve immediately.

ingredients

14 oz/400 g lean pork fillet
3 tbsp orange marmalade
grated rind and juice of 1 orange
1 tbsp white wine vinegar
dash of Tabasco sauce
salt and pepper

sauce
1 tbsp olive oil
1 small onion, chopped
1 small green bell pepper, deseeded
  and thinly sliced
1 tbsp cornstarch
2/3 cup/5 fl oz orange juice

to serve
cooked rice
mixed salad leaves

tangy pork fillet

SERVES	PREP	COOK
4	**10** mins	**55** mins

Barbecued in a parcel of kitchen foil, these tasty pork fillets are served with a tangy orange sauce.

1 Place a large piece of double thickness foil in a shallow dish. Put the pork fillet in the center of the foil and season.

2 Heat the marmalade, orange rind, and juice, vinegar, and Tabasco sauce in a small pan, stirring until the marmalade melts and the ingredients combine. Pour the mixture over the pork and wrap the meat in foil, making sure that the package is well sealed so that the juices cannot run out. Place over hot coals and barbecue for about 25 minutes, turning the package occasionally.

3 For the sauce, heat the oil in a pan and cook the onion for 2–3 minutes. Add the bell pepper and cook for 3–4 minutes.

4 Remove the pork from the kitchen foil and place on to the rack. Pour the juices into the pan with the sauce.

5 Barbecue the pork for a further 10–20 minutes, turning, until cooked through and golden on the outside.

6 In a small bowl, mix the cornstarch with a little orange juice to form a paste. Add to the sauce with the remaining cooking juices. Cook, stirring, until the sauce thickens. Slice the pork, spoon over the sauce and serve with rice and mixed green salad.

frankly fabulous skewers

SERVES	PREP	COOK
4	**10** mins	**40** mins

A new way with an old favorite—cook frankfurter sausages on the barbecue for a wonderful smoky flavor and an incredibly easy meal. They are served here with garlic toast.

1 Preheat the barbecue. To make the garlic toast, slice off the tops of the garlic bulbs. Brush the bulbs with oil and wrap them in foil. Cook over hot coals, turning occasionally, for 30 minutes.

2 Meanwhile, cut each frankfurter sausage into 3 pieces. Thread the frankfurter pieces, zucchini slices, corn slices, cherry tomatoes, and pearl onions alternately onto metal skewers. Brush with olive oil.

3 Cook the skewers over hot coals, turning and brushing frequently with the oil, for 8–10 minutes. Meanwhile, brush the slices of baguette with oil and toast both sides on the barbecue. Unwrap the garlic bulbs and squeeze the cloves onto the bread. Season to taste with salt and pepper and drizzle over a little extra olive oil, if you like. Transfer the skewers to a large serving plate and serve immediately with the garlic toast.

ingredients

12 frankfurter sausages
2 zucchinis, cut into $^1/_2$-inch/
  1-cm slices
2 corn ears, cut into $^1/_2$-inch/
  1-cm slices
12 cherry tomatoes
12 pearl onions
2 tbsp olive oil

garlic toast
2 garlic bulbs
2–3 tbsp olive oil
1 baguette, sliced
salt and pepper

soy pork with coriander

SERVES
4

PREP
10
mins

+1hr
marinating

COOK
14-20
mins

The spicy, Eastern-style flavors that suffuse these pork chops will make them an unusual and original barbecue favorite.

1 Place the pork chops in a large, shallow, nonmetallic dish. Crush the coriander seeds and peppercorns in a spice mill. Alternatively, place in a mortar and crush with a pestle. Place the soy sauce, garlic, sugar, crushed coriander seeds, and peppercorns in a measuring cup and stir well until the sugar has dissolved.

2 Pour the soy sauce mixture over the chops, turning to coat. Cover with plastic wrap and let marinate in the refrigerator for 1 hour, turning occasionally.

3 Preheat the barbecue. Drain the chops, reserving the marinade. Cook over medium hot coals, brushing frequently with the reserved marinade, for 7–10 minutes on each side. Transfer to a large serving plate, garnish with fresh cilantro sprigs, and serve.

ingredients

4 pork chops, about 6 oz/
  175 g each
1 tbsp coriander seeds
6 black peppercorns
4 tbsp dark soy sauce
1 garlic clove, finely chopped
1 tsp sugar

to garnish
fresh cilantro sprigs

herbed pork chops with blue cheese and walnut butter

SERVES	PREP		COOK
4	**10** mins	**+12 hrs** marinating	**35-40** mins

The flavored butter adds a wonderfully rich taste to the barbecued chops as it melts.

1 Trim the fat from the chops and place them in a dish. Whisk together the oil, lemon juice, marjoram, thyme, parsley, garlic, and onion in a bowl, then season with salt and pepper. Pour the marinade over the chops, turning to coat. Cover and let marinate in the refrigerator overnight.

2 To make the flavored butter, melt half the butter in a skillet, and cook the scallions over low heat, stirring frequently for a few minutes, until softened. Transfer to a bowl and mix in the remaining butter, the cheese, and walnuts. Form into a roll, then cover and let chill until required.

3 Drain the chops, reserving the marinade. Grill the chops on a hot barbecue for 5 minutes on each side, then grill over more medium coals or on a higher rack, turning and brushing occasionally with the reserved marinade, for about 10 minutes more on each side, or until cooked through and tender. Transfer to serving plates and top each chop with 1–2 slices of the cheese and walnut butter. Serve at once with a small salad.

ingredients

4 pork chops

marinade
4 tbsp corn oil
2 tbsp lemon juice
1 tbsp chopped fresh marjoram
1 tbsp chopped fresh thyme
2 tablespoons chopped fresh
  parsley
1 garlic clove, finely chopped
1 onion, finely chopped
salt and pepper

blue cheese and walnut butter
2 oz/55 g butter
4 scallions, finely chopped
5 oz/140 g Gorgonzola cheese,
  crumbled
2 tbsp finely chopped walnuts

to serve
small salad

pork & apple skewers

SERVES	PREP	COOK
4	10 mins	15 mins

Flavored with mustard and served with a mustard sauce, these kabobs make an ideal lunch.

1 To make the mustard sauce, combine the wholegrain and Dijon-style mustards in a small bowl and slowly blend in the cream. Leave to stand until required.

2 Cut the pork fillet into bite-size pieces and set aside until required.

3 Core the apples, then cut them into thick wedges. Toss the apple wedges in a little lemon juice—this will prevent any discoloration. Slice the lemon.

4 Thread the pork, apple, and lemon slices alternately on to 4 metal or pre-soaked wooden skewers.

5 Mix together the mustards, apple or orange juice, and sunflower oil. Brush the mixture over the kabobs and barbecue over hot coals for 10–15 minutes, until cooked through, frequently turning and basting the kabobs with the mustard marinade.

6 Transfer the kabobs to warm serving dishes and spoon over a little of the mustard sauce. Serve the kabobs with fresh, crusty brown bread.

ingredients

1 lb/450 g pork fillet
2 eating apples
a little lemon juice
1 lemon
2 tsp wholegrain mustard
2 tsp Dijon-style mustard
2 tbsp apple or orange juice
2 tbsp sunflower oil

mustard sauce
1 tbsp wholegrain mustard
1 tsp Dijon-style mustard
6 tbsp light cream

to serve
crusty brown bread

kabobtasty tangy sumptuousfillet juicy brochettestender...

lamb

minted lamb chops

 SERVES 6

 PREP 15 mins

+2hrs marinating

 COOK 10-14 mins

You can prepare this dish with any kind of lamb chops, such as loin chops or leg chops, which are especially tender. Shoulder steaks also work well in this recipe.

1 Place the chops in a large, shallow, nonmetallic bowl. Mix half the yogurt, the garlic, ginger, and coriander seeds together in a measuring cup and season to taste with salt and pepper. Spoon the mixture over the chops, turning to coat, then cover with plastic wrap and let marinate in the refrigerator for 2 hours, turning occasionally.

2 Preheat the barbecue. Place the remaining yogurt, the olive oil, orange juice, walnut oil, and mint in a small bowl and, using a hand-held whisk, whisk until thoroughly blended. Season to taste with salt and pepper. Cover the minted yogurt with plastic wrap and let chill in the refrigerator until ready to serve.

3 Drain the chops, scraping off the marinade. Brush with olive oil and cook over medium hot coals for 5–7 minutes on each side. Serve immediately with the minted yogurt.

ingredients

6 chump chops, about 6 oz/
  175 g each
$^2/_3$ cup strained plain yogurt
2 garlic cloves, finely chopped
1 tsp grated fresh gingerroot
$^1/_4$ tsp coriander seeds, crushed
salt and pepper
1 tbsp olive oil, plus extra for
  brushing
1 tbsp orange juice
1 tsp walnut oil
2 tbsp chopped fresh mint

moroccan lamb kabobs

SERVES	PREP	+2-8 hrs	COOK
4	25 mins	marinating	10 mins

Marinated in Moroccan spices, these grilled kebabs have a mild spicy flavor. Add the chili if you like a bit of zip to your meat.

1 Cut the lamb into large, evenly-sized pieces.

2 To make the marinade, combine the lemon rind and juice, oil, garlic, chili (if using), ground cinnamon, ginger, cumin, and coriander in a large non-metallic dish.

3 Add the meat to the marinade, tossing to coat the meat completely. Cover and leave to marinate in the refrigerator for at least 2 hours or preferably overnight.

4 Cut the lemon into 8 pieces. Cut the onion into wedges, then separate each wedge into 2 pieces.

5 Using a potato peeler, cut thin strips of peel from the zucchini, then cut the zucchini into chunks.

6 Remove the meat from the marinade, reserving the liquid for basting. Thread the meat on to skewers alternating with the onion, lemon, and zucchini.

7 Grill over hot coals for 8–10 minutes, turning and basting with the reserved marinade. Serve on a bed of couscous.

ingredients

1 lb/450 g lean lamb
1 lemon
1 red onion
4 small zucchini

marinade
grated rind and juice of 1 lemon
2 tbsp olive oil
1 clove garlic, crushed
1 red chili, sliced (optional)
1 tsp ground cinnamon
1 tsp ground ginger
$^1/_2$ tsp ground cumin
$^1/_2$ tsp ground coriander

to serve
couscous

rack & ruin

SERVES	PREP		COOK
4	10 hrs	+1hr marinating	20 mins

This quick and easy dish is perfect for serving as part of a summer party menu, along with plenty of salad and potatoes.

1 Place the racks of lamb in a large, shallow, nonmetallic dish. Place the oil, vinegar, lemon juice, rosemary, and onion in a measuring cup and stir together. Season to taste with salt and pepper.

2 Pour the marinade over the lamb and turn until thoroughly coated. Cover with plastic wrap and let marinate in the refrigerator for 1 hour, turning occasionally.

3 Preheat the barbecue. Drain the racks of lamb, reserving the marinade. Cook over medium hot coals, brushing frequently with the marinade, for 10 minutes on each side. Serve immediately.

ingredients

4 racks of lamb, each with
  4 chops
2 tbsp extra-virgin olive oil
1 tbsp balsamic vinegar
1 tbsp lemon juice
3 tbsp finely chopped fresh
  rosemary
1 small onion, finely chopped
salt and pepper

sozzled lamb chops

SERVES	PREP		COOK
4	**15** mins	**+5 mins** marinating	**10** mins

These chops will only need marinating for a short time, as the marinade is quite strongly flavored. They are delicious served with a rich, tasty mustard butter.

1 Preheat the barbecue. Place the lamb chops in a large, shallow, nonmetallic dish. Mix all the ingredients for the marinade together in a measuring cup, seasoning to taste with salt and pepper. Pour the mixture over the chops and then turn them until they are well coated. Cover with plastic wrap and let marinate for 5 minutes.

2 To make the mustard butter, mix all the ingredients together in a small bowl, beating with a fork until well blended. Cover with plastic wrap and let chill in the refrigerator until required.

3 Drain the chops, reserving the marinade. Cook over medium hot coals, brushing frequently with the reserved marinade, for 5 minutes on each side. Transfer to serving plates, top with the mustard butter, and garnish with parsley sprigs. Serve immediately with salad.

ingredients

8 lamb loin chops

marinade
2 tbsp extra-virgin olive oil
2 tbsp Worcestershire sauce
2 tbsp lemon juice
2 tbsp dry gin
1 garlic clove, finely chopped
salt and pepper

mustard butter
2 oz/55 g unsalted butter, softened
$1^1/_2$ tsp tarragon mustard
1 tbsp chopped fresh parsley
dash of lemon juice

to garnish
fresh parsley sprigs

to serve
salad

lamb burgers with mint & pine nuts

SERVES
4

PREP
15
mins

+30 mins
chilling

COOK
5-10
mins

These tasty burgers have a Greek flavor. Serve them in the traditional warmed pita breads or in soft buns with salad greens.

1 Place the ground lamb, chopped onion, pine nuts, fresh mint, and salt and pepper to taste in a large bowl and mix together until thoroughly combined. Using your hands, divide the mixture into 4 and shape the portions into round burgers, pressing the mixture together well. Let chill in the refrigerator for 30 minutes.

2 Preheat the barbecue. Cook the burgers over hot coals for 4–5 minutes on each side, turning once, until the juices run clear.

3 Warm the pita breads at the side of the grill or toast the buns. Crumble the feta cheese into small pieces and reserve until required.

4 Line the pita bread or buns with the salad greens. Sandwich the burgers between the pita bread or buns and top with the crumbled feta cheese.

ingredients

1 lb/450 g fresh lean ground lamb
1 small onion, finely chopped
scant $1/2$ cup pine nuts
2 tbsp chopped fresh mint
salt and pepper

to serve
4 pita breads or soft buns
$2^3/4$ oz/75 g feta cheese
salad greens

sweet lamb fillet

SERVES	PREP	COOK
4	5 mins	1 hr

Lamb fillet, enhanced by a sweet and spicy glaze, is cooked on the grill in a kitchen foil parcel for deliciously moist results.

1 Place the lamb fillet on a large piece of double thickness kitchen foil. Season with salt and pepper to taste.

2 Heat the oil in a small pan and fry the onion and garlic for 2–3 minutes until softened but not browned. Stir in the grated ginger and cook for 1 minute, stirring occasionally.

3 Stir in the apple juice, apple sauce, sugar, catsup and mustard and bring to the boil. Boil rapidly for about 10 minutes until reduced by half. Stir the mixture occasionally so that it does not burn and stick to the base of the pan.

4 Brush half of the sauce over the lamb, then wrap up the lamb in the kitchen foil to completely enclose it. Cook the lamb parcels over hot coals for about 25 minutes, turning the parcel over occasionally.

5 Open out the kitchen foil and brush the lamb with some of the sauce. Continue to cook for a further 15–20 minutes or until cooked through.

6 Place the lamb on a chopping board, remove the foil and cut into thick slices. Transfer to serving plates and spoon over the remaining sauce. Serve with green salad leaves, croûtons and fresh crusty bread.

ingredients

2 fillets of neck of lean lamb, each 8 oz/225 g
1 tbsp olive oil
$1/2$ onion, chopped finely
1 clove garlic, crushed
2.5 cm/1 inch piece fresh ginger, grated
5 tbsp apple juice
3 tbsp smooth apple sauce
1 tbsp light muscovado sugar
1 tbsp tomato catsup
$1/2$ tsp mild mustard
salt and pepper

to serve
green salad leaves, croûtons and fresh crusty bread

ingredients

marinade
2 tsp vegetable oil
1 tsp curry powder
1 tsp garam masala
2 tsp granulated sugar
scant 1 cup plain yogurt

skewers
14 oz/400 g boneless lamb, cubed
scant 1 cup dried apricot halves
1 red or green bell pepper, seeded
  and cut into small chunks
2 zucchini, cubed
16 pearl onions

to garnish
fresh cilantro leaves

to serve
freshly steamed or boiled rice
crisp salad greens

curried lamb skewers

SERVES	PREP		COOK
4	10 mins	**+8hrs** marinating	15-20 mins

A subtle combination of flavors makes this a stylish dish for a barbecue.

1 Put the oil, spices, sugar, and yogurt into a large bowl and mix until well combined.

2 Thread the lamb onto 8 skewers, alternating it with the apricot halves, red bell pepper, zucchini, and pearl onions. When the skewers are full (leave a small space at either end), transfer them to the bowl, and turn them in the yogurt mixture until they are well coated. Cover with plastic wrap and place in the refrigerator to marinate for at least 8 hours or overnight.

3 When the skewers are thoroughly marinated, lift them out, and barbecue them over hot coals, turning them frequently, for 15 minutes, or until the meat is cooked right through. Serve at once with freshly cooked rice or crisp salad greens, garnished with fresh cilantro leaves.

lamb and wild mushroom brochettes

SERVES	PREP		COOK
6	**15** mins	**+4hrs** marinating	**15-20** mins

The earthy flavor of wild mushrooms goes well with the sweetness of lamb.

1 Pour the wine, olive oil, and lemon juice into a large, shallow dish and season with salt and pepper. Stir in the onion, garlic, and thyme, then add the lamb and stir again to coat. Cover with plastic wrap and let marinate in the refrigerator for 4 hours.

2 Drain the lamb, reserving the marinade. Loosely roll up the bacon slices. Thread the cubes of lamb, bacon rolls, and mushrooms alternately onto 6 long skewers and finish each with a cherry tomato.

3 Brush the brochettes generously with the reserved marinade. Grill on a medium barbecue, turning and brushing occasionally with the marinade, for about 15 minutes, or until cooked through and tender. Garnish with fresh rosemary, and serve immediately, with a rice salad.

ingredients

$^1/_2$ cup red wine
6 tbsp olive oil
1 tbsp lemon juice
salt and pepper
1 large onion, chopped
2 garlic cloves, finely chopped
1 tbsp chopped fresh thyme
2 lb 4 oz/1 kg boned leg of lamb,
  cut into 1-inch/2.5-cm cubes
12 slices lean bacon, rinds
  removed
24 wild mushrooms
6 cherry tomatoes

to garnish
rosemary sprigs

to serve
rice salad

spicy lamb steaks

SERVES	PREP	+3hrs 20mins	COOK
4	15 mins	cooling/ marinating	40 mins

Lamb, fresh rosemary, and bay leaves always go so well together, and in this delicious dish a hot and spicy marinade is used to give the lamb an extra special flavor.

1 To make the marinade, heat the oil in a heavy-bottom pan. Add the onion and garlic and cook, stirring occasionally, for 5 minutes, or until softened. Stir in the jerk seasoning, curry paste, and grated ginger, and cook, stirring constantly, for 2 minutes. Add the tomatoes, Worcestershire sauce, and sugar, then season to taste with salt and pepper. Bring to a boil, stirring constantly, then reduce the heat and let simmer for 15 minutes, or until thickened. Remove from the heat and let cool.

2 Place the lamb steaks between 2 sheets of plastic wrap and beat with the side of a rolling pin to flatten. Transfer the steaks to a large, shallow, nonmetallic dish. Pour the marinade over them, turning to coat. Cover with plastic wrap and let marinate in the refrigerator for 3 hours.

3 Preheat the barbecue. Drain the lamb, reserving the marinade. Cook the lamb over medium hot coals, brushing frequently with the marinade, for 5–7 minutes on each side. Meanwhile, dip the rosemary and bay leaves in the olive oil and cook on the barbecue for 3–5 minutes. Serve the lamb immediately with the herbs.

ingredients

4 lamb steaks, about 6 oz/175 g each
8 fresh rosemary sprigs
8 fresh bay leaves
2 tbsp olive oil

spicy marinade
2 tbsp corn oil
1 large onion, finely chopped
2 garlic cloves, finely chopped
2 tbsp Jamaican jerk seasoning
1 tbsp curry paste
1 tsp grated fresh gingerroot
14 oz/400 g canned chopped tomatoes
4 tbsp Worcestershire sauce
3 tbsp light brown sugar
salt and pepper

turkish kabobs

SERVES	PREP		COOK
4	**20** mins	**+2hrs** marinating	**10-15** mins

Turkey, the bridge between East and West, has an eclectic mix of influences in its cooking style. These traditional kabobs would originally have been made with mutton or, possibly, young goat.

ingredients

1 lb 2 oz/500 g boned shoulder
 of lamb, cut into 1-inch/
 2.5-cm cubes
1 tbsp olive oil
2 tbsp dry white wine
2 tbsp finely chopped fresh mint
4 garlic cloves, finely chopped
2 tsp grated orange rind
1 tbsp paprika
1 tsp sugar
salt and pepper

sesame seed cream
8 oz/225 g sesame seed paste
2 garlic cloves, finely chopped
2 tbsp extra-virgin olive oil
2 tbsp lemon juice
$^1/_2$ cup water

1 Place the lamb cubes in a large, shallow, nonmetallic dish. Mix the olive oil, wine, mint, garlic, orange rind, paprika, and sugar together in a measuring cup and season to taste with salt and pepper. Pour the mixture over the lamb, turning to coat, then cover and let marinate in the refrigerator for 2 hours, turning occasionally.

2 Preheat the barbecue. To make the sesame seed cream, put the sesame seed paste, garlic, oil, and lemon juice into a food processor and process briefly to mix. With the motor still running, gradually add the water through the feeder tube until smooth. Transfer to a bowl, cover, and let chill in the refrigerator until required.

3 Drain the lamb, reserving the marinade, and thread it onto several long metal skewers. Cook over medium hot coals, turning and brushing frequently with the reserved marinade, for 10–15 minutes. Serve with the sesame seed cream.

butterfly lamb with balsamic vinegar & mint

SERVES	PREP		COOK
4	**20** mins	**+6hrs** marinating	**1** hrs

The appearance of the leg of lamb as it is opened out to cook on the barbecue gives this dish its name.

1 Open out the boned leg of lamb so that its shape resembles a butterfly. Thread 2–3 skewers through the meat to make it easier to turn on the grill.

2 Mix the balsamic vinegar, lemon rind and juice, corn oil, mint, garlic, sugar, and salt and pepper to taste together in a nonmetallic dish that is large enough to hold the lamb. Place the lamb in the dish and turn it over a few times so that the meat is coated on both sides with the marinade. Cover and let marinate in the refrigerator for at least 6 hours, or preferably overnight, turning occasionally.

3 Preheat the barbecue. Remove the lamb from the marinade and reserve the liquid for basting. Place the rack about 6 inches/ 15 cm above the coals and cook the lamb for 30 minutes on each side, turning once and basting frequently with the marinade.

4 Transfer the lamb to a cutting board and remove the skewers. Cut the lamb into slices across the grain and serve with broiled vegetables and salad greens.

ingredients

boned leg of lamb, about
  4 lb/1.8 kg
scant $^1/_2$ cup balsamic vinegar
grated rind and juice of 1 lemon
$^2/_3$ cup corn oil
4 tbsp chopped fresh mint
2 garlic cloves, crushed
2 tbsp brown sugar
salt and pepper

to serve
broiled vegetables
salad greens

lamb and feta cheese burgers

SERVES	PREP	+30 mins	COOK
4-6	**10** mins	chilling	**8** mins

ingredients

1 lb/450 g fresh ground lamb
8 oz/225 g feta cheese,
  crumbled
2 garlic cloves, crushed
6 scallions, finely chopped
$1/2$ cup no-soak prunes, chopped
2 tbsp pine nuts, toasted
1 cup fresh whole-wheat bread
  crumbs
1 tbsp chopped fresh rosemary
salt and pepper
1 tbsp corn oil

These burgers are absolutely delicious—the combination of the feta cheese with the prunes, pine nuts, and rosemary may sound rather unusual, but tastes fabulous.

1 Place the ground lamb in a large bowl with the cheese, garlic, scallions, prunes, pine nuts, and bread crumbs. Mix well, breaking up any lumps of meat.

2 Add the rosemary and salt and pepper to the lamb mixture in the bowl. Mix together, then shape into 4–6 equal-size burgers. Cover and let chill for 30 minutes.

3 Preheat the barbecue. Brush the burgers lightly with oil and cook over hot coals for 4 minutes before turning over and brushing with the remaining oil. Continue to cook for 4 minutes, or until cooked to personal preference. Serve.

persian lamb

SERVES	PREP	+2–3 hrs	COOK
4-6	15 hrs	marinating	25 mins

Chargrilling and lamb seem to be made for each other, and all over the Middle East both lamb and mutton are enjoyed in this way.

1 For the marinade, combine the mint, yogurt, garlic, and pepper.

2 Put the cutlets into a non-porous dish and rub all over with the lemon juice. Pour the marinade over the cutlets. Cover and marinate for 2–3 hours.

3 To make the tabbouleh, put the couscous into a heatproof bowl and pour over the boiling water. Leave for 5 minutes. Drain and put into a strainer. Steam over a pan of barely simmering water for 8 minutes. Toss in the oil and lemon juice. Add the onion, tomato and herbs. Season and set aside.

4 Cook the lamb over a medium grill for 15 minutes, turning once. Serve with the tabbouleh.

ingredients

2 tbsp chopped fresh mint
1 cup lowfat plain yogurt
4 garlic cloves, crushed
$1/4$ tsp pepper
6 lean lamb cutlets
2 tbsp lemon juice

tabbouleh
2 cups couscous
2 cups boiling water
2 tbsp olive oil
2 tbsp lemon juice
$1/2$ onion, minced
4 tomatoes, minced
$1/2$ cup fresh cilantro, chopped
2 tbsp chopped fresh mint
salt and pepper

lemon & herb kabobs

SERVES	PREP		COOK
4	20 mins	+8hrs marinating	10-15 mins

These fragrant, lemon–flavored kabobs, are a Georgian speciality from the fertile area between the Black Sea and the Caucasian Mountains in the Russian Federation.

1 Place the lamb and mushrooms in a large, shallow, nonmetallic dish. Mix all the ingredients for the marinade together in a measuring cup, seasoning to taste with salt and pepper. Pour the mixture over the lamb and mushrooms, turning to coat. Cover with plastic wrap and let marinate in the refrigerator for up to 8 hours.

2 Preheat the barbecue. Cut the bacon strips in half across the center and stretch with a heavy, flat-bladed knife, then roll up. Drain the lamb and mushrooms, reserving the marinade. Thread the bacon rolls, lamb, mushrooms, tomatoes, and bell pepper squares alternately onto metal skewers. Strain the marinade.

3 Cook the kabobs over medium hot coals, turning and brushing frequently with the reserved marinade, for 10–15 minutes. Transfer to a large serving plate, garnish with fresh herb sprigs, and serve immediately.

ingredients

1 lb 8 oz/675 g boneless leg of lamb, cut into 1-inch/2.5-cm cubes
12 large mushrooms
4 lean bacon strips, rinded
8 cherry tomatoes
1 large green bell pepper, seeded and cut into squares

marinade
4 tbsp corn oil
4 tbsp lemon juice
1 onion, finely chopped
$1/2$ tsp dried rosemary
$1/2$ tsp dried thyme
salt and pepper

to garnish
fresh herb sprigs

chickenwingsspicymarinadeyumyumjuicy
duckdrumsticks...

poultry

mustard & honey drumsticks

SERVES	PREP		COOK
4	**10** mins	**+1hr** marinating	**25–30** mins

Chicken can taste rather bland, but this sweet-and-sour glaze gives it a wonderful piquancy and helps to keep it moist during cooking.

1 Using a sharp knife, make 2–3 diagonal slashes in the chicken drumsticks and place them in a large, nonmetallic dish.

2 Mix all the ingredients for the glaze together in a measuring cup and season to taste with salt and pepper. Pour the glaze over the drumsticks, turning until the drumsticks are well coated. Cover with plastic wrap and let marinate in the refrigerator for at least 1 hour.

3 Preheat the barbecue. Drain the chicken drumsticks, reserving the marinade. Cook the chicken over medium hot coals, turning frequently and brushing with the reserved marinade, for 25–30 minutes, or until thoroughly cooked. Transfer to serving plates, garnish with fresh parsley sprigs, and serve immediately with salad.

ingredients

8 chicken drumsticks

glaze
$^1/_2$ cup honey
4 tbsp Dijon mustard
4 tbsp whole-grain mustard
4 tbsp white wine vinegar
2 tbsp corn oil
salt and pepper

to garnish
fresh parsley sprigs

to serve
salad

the ultimate chicken burger

SERVES	PREP	+30	COOK
4	**10** mins	**mins** chilling	**15-20** mins

ingredients

4 large chicken breast fillets, skinned
1 large egg white
1 tbsp cornstarch
1 tbsp all-purpose flour
1 egg, beaten
1 cup fresh white bread crumbs
2 tbsp corn oil
2 beefsteak tomatoes, sliced

These deliciously thin pieces of breaded chicken, served in a classic sesame seed bun with ketchup or mayonnaise, will go down very well with all the chicken and burger enthusiasts you know.

1 Place the chicken breasts between 2 sheets of nonstick parchment paper and flatten slightly using a meat mallet or a rolling pin. Beat the egg white and cornstarch together, then brush over the chicken. Cover and let chill for 30 minutes, then coat in the flour.

2 Place the egg and bread crumbs in 2 separate bowls and coat the burgers first in the egg, allowing any excess to drip back into the bowl, then in the bread crumbs.

3 Preheat the barbecue. When hot, add the burgers and cook over hot coals for 6–8 minutes on each side, or until thoroughly cooked. If you are in doubt, it is worth cutting one of the burgers in half. If there is any sign of pinkness, cook for a little longer. Add the tomato slices for the last 1–2 minutes of the cooking time to heat through. Serve.

zesty kabobs

SERVES 4

PREP 10 mins +8hrs marinating

COOK 6-10 mins

These lovely, fresh-tasting chicken kabobs are marinated in a zingy mixture of citrus juice and rind. They are very easy to make and make a perfect main course for a barbecue party.

1 Using a sharp knife, cut the chicken into 1-inch/2.5-cm cubes, then place them in a large glass bowl. Place the lemon and orange rind, the lemon and orange juice, the honey, oil, mint, and ground coriander in a measuring cup and mix together. Season to taste with salt and pepper. Pour the marinade over the chicken cubes and toss until thoroughly coated. Cover with plastic wrap and let marinate in the refrigerator for up to 8 hours.

2 Preheat the barbecue. Drain the chicken cubes, reserving the marinade. Thread the chicken onto several long metal skewers.

3 Cook the skewers over medium hot coals, turning and brushing frequently with the reserved marinade, for 6–10 minutes, or until thoroughly cooked. Transfer to a large serving plate, garnish with fresh mint sprigs and citrus zest, and serve immediately.

ingredients

4 skinless, boneless chicken
  breasts, about 6 oz/175 g each
finely grated rind and juice of
  $1/2$ lemon
finely grated rind and juice of
  $1/2$ orange
2 tbsp honey
2 tbsp olive oil
2 tbsp chopped fresh mint
$1/4$ tsp ground coriander
salt and pepper

to garnish
fresh mint sprigs
citrus zest

pesto and ricotta chicken with tomato vinaigrette

SERVES 4

PREP 15 mins

+30 mins chilling

COOK 20 mins

ingredients

1 tbsp pesto sauce
$^1/_2$ cup ricotta cheese
4 x 6 oz/175 g skinless, boneless
  chicken breasts
1 tbsp olive oil
pepper

to garnish
small salad

tomato vinaigrette
generous $^1/_3$ cup olive oil
1 bunch fresh chives
1 lb 2 oz/500 g tomatoes, peeled,
  seeded, and chopped
juice and finely grated rind of
  1 lime
salt and pepper

The flavors and aromas of the Mediterranean turn a simple piece of chicken into a summer feast.

1 Mix together the pesto and ricotta in a small bowl until well combined. Using a sharp knife, cut a deep slit in the side of each chicken breast to make a pocket. Spoon the ricotta mixture into the pockets and reshape the chicken breasts to enclose it. Place the chicken on a plate, cover, and let chill for 30 minutes.

2 To make the vinaigrette, pour the olive oil into a blender or food processor, add the chives, and process until smooth. Scrape the mixture into a bowl and stir in the tomatoes, lime juice, and rind. Season to taste with salt and pepper.

3 Brush the chicken with the olive oil and season with pepper. Grill on a fairly hot barbecue for about 8 minutes on each side, or until cooked through and tender. Transfer to serving plates, spoon over the vinaigrette, and serve at once.

duck breasts with maple syrup and cranberry relish

ingredients

4 duck breasts, about 8 oz/
  225 g each
4 tbsp maple syrup
juice and finely grated rind
  of 1 orange
juice and finely grated rind
  of 1 lemon

cranberry relish

2 cups fresh or frozen cranberries
2 shallots, finely chopped
$^2/_3$ cup red wine
generous $^1/_2$ cup superfine sugar
2 tsp cornstarch
juice and finely grated rind
  of 1 orange
1 tsp ground allspice

SERVES	PREP	+30	COOK
4	**10** mins	**mins** chilling	**35** mins

The slight sharpness of the relish contrasts delightfully with the sweet glaze and rich meat.

1 For the relish, put the cranberries, shallots, wine, and sugar into a pan and bring to a boil, stirring. Reduce the heat and let simmer for 10–15 minutes, until soft. Mix together the cornstarch, orange juice, and allspice in a small bowl, then stir into the cranberries. Add the orange rind and cook, stirring, until thickened. Remove from the heat, cover, and let cool, then let chill until ready to serve.

2 Cut off any excess fat from the duck breasts and score the skin. Cut the duck breasts into 1-inch/2.5-cm cubes and thread onto skewers. Mix together the maple syrup, orange juice and rind, and lemon juice and rind in a bowl.

3 Grill the duck breasts over hot coals for 2 minutes on each side, then brush with the maple syrup mixture. Grill, turning and brushing with the maple syrup mixture frequently, for about 8 minutes, or until cooked through and tender. Serve at once, with the cranberry relish.

jerk chicken

| SERVES 4 | PREP 15 mins | +24hrs marinating | COOK 30 mins |

ingredients

4 lean chicken portions
1 bunch scallions, trimmed
1–2 chili peppers (Scotch Bonnet, if possible)
1 garlic clove
2 inch/5 cm piece fresh ginger, peeled and roughly chopped
$^1/_2$ tsp dried thyme
$^1/_2$ tsp paprika
$^1/_4$ tsp ground allspice
pinch ground cinnamon
pinch ground cloves
4 tbsp white wine vinegar
3 tbsp light soy sauce
pepper

This is perhaps one of the best known Caribbean dishes. The "jerk" in the name refers to the hot spicy coating.

1 Rinse the chicken portions and pat them dry on absorbent kitchen paper. Place them in a shallow dish.

2 Place the scallions, chili peppers, garlic, ginger, thyme, paprika, allspice, cinnamon, cloves, wine vinegar, soy sauce, and pepper to taste in a food processor and process until smooth.

3 Pour the spicy mixture over the chicken. Turn the chicken portions over so that they are well coated in the marinade.

4 Transfer the chicken portions to the refrigerator and leave to marinate for up to 24 hours.

5 Remove the chicken from the marinade and grill over medium hot coals for about 30 minutes, turning the chicken over and basting occasionally with any remaining marinade, until the chicken is browned and cooked through.

6 Transfer the chicken portions to individual serving plates and serve at once.

chicken skewers with lemon & cilantro

SERVES
4

PREP
10
mins

+2hrs
marinating

COOK
15
mins

These tasty and tender chicken kabobs are perfect served as part of a barbecue lunch party with plenty of crisp salad greens and a delicious lemon yogurt dressing.

1 Using a sharp knife, cut the chicken into 2.5-cm/1-inch pieces and place in a shallow, nonmetallic dish.

2 Add the ground coriander, lemon juice, salt and pepper to taste, and 4 tablespoons of the yogurt to the chicken and mix together with a wooden spoon until thoroughly combined. Cover with plastic wrap and let chill in the refrigerator for at least 2 hours, preferably overnight.

3 Preheat the barbecue. To make the lemon yogurt, peel and finely chop the lemon, discarding any seeds. Stir the lemon into the remaining yogurt together with the chopped cilantro. Chill in the refrigerator until required.

4 Thread the chicken pieces on to several presoaked wooden skewers. Brush the rack with corn oil and cook the chicken over hot coals for 15 minutes, basting with the oil.

5 Transfer the chicken skewers to warmed serving plates and garnish with cilantro sprigs and lemon wedges. Serve the skewers with a selection of salad greens and the lemon yogurt.

ingredients

4 skinless, boneless chicken
  breasts
1 tsp ground coriander
2 tsp lemon juice
salt and pepper
$1^1/_4$ cups plain yogurt
1 lemon
2 tbsp chopped fresh cilantro
corn oil, for brushing

to serve
salad greens

to garnish
fresh cilantro sprigs
lemon wedges

barbecued chicken legs

SERVES	PREP	COOK
4	**5** mins	**20** mins

ingredients

12 chicken drumsticks

spiced butter
³/₄ cup butter
2 garlic cloves, crushed
1 tsp grated ginger root
2 tsp ground turmeric
4 tsp cayenne pepper
2 tbsp lime juice
3 tbsp mango chutney

to serve
crisp green salad
boiled rice

Just the thing to put on the barbecue—chicken legs, coated with a spicy, curry-like butter, then grilled until crispy and golden.

1 To make the Spiced Butter mixture, beat the butter with the garlic, ginger, turmeric, cayenne pepper, lime juice and chutney until well blended.

2 Using a sharp knife, slash each chicken leg to the bone 3-4 times.

3 Cook the drumsticks over medium hot coals for about 12-15 minutes or until almost cooked.

4 Brush the chicken legs thickly with the butter mixture and continue to cook for a further 5-6 minutes, turning and basting frequently with the butter until golden and crisp. Serve the chicken legs hot or cold with a crisp green salad and rice.

hot red chicken

SERVES	PREP		COOK
4	**10** mins	**+8hrs** marinating	**25-30** mins

In this adaptation of a traditional Indian recipe for spring chickens, chicken pieces are used, and they are just as tasty.

1 Place the curry paste, tomato ketchup, five-spice powder, chili Worcestershire sauce, and sugar in a small bowl, and stir until the sugar has dissolved. Season to taste with salt.

2 Place the chicken pieces in a large, shallow, nonmetallic dish and spoon the spice paste over them, rubbing it in well. Cover with plastic wrap and let marinate in the refrigerator for up to 8 hours.

3 Preheat the barbecue. Remove the chicken from the spice paste, discarding any remaining paste, and brush with oil. Cook the chicken over medium hot coals, turning occasionally, for 25–30 minutes. Briefly heat the naan bread on the barbecue and serve with the chicken, garnished with lemon wedges and cilantro sprigs.

ingredients

1 tbsp curry paste
1 tbsp tomato ketchup
1 tsp five-spice powder
1 fresh red chili, seeded and
  finely chopped
1 tsp Worcestershire sauce
1 tsp sugar
salt
8 skinless chicken pieces
vegetable oil, for brushing

to serve
naan bread

to garnish
lemon wedges
fresh cilantro sprigs

maple-glazed turkey burgers

SERVES **4**

PREP **15** mins

+1hr chilling

COOK **16-19** mins

ingredients

2 ears fresh corn with leaves
  intact
1 lb/450 g fresh ground turkey
1 red bell pepper, seeded,
  peeled, and finely chopped
6 scallions, finely chopped
1 cup fresh white bread crumbs
2 tbsp chopped fresh basil
salt and pepper
1 tbsp corn oil
2 tbsp maple syrup

To give the meal an authentic taste of the American deep south, serve these burgers with corn fritters and sautéed banana. When cooking bananas toss in lemon juice to help preserve their color.

1 Preheat the barbecue and when up to temperature add the ears of fresh corn, and cook over medium-high heat for 8–10 minutes, turning every 2–3 minutes, or until the leaves are charred. Remove from the barbecue rack, let cool, then strip off the leaves and silky threads. Using a sharp knife, cut away the kernels and place in a bowl.

2 Add the ground turkey, red bell pepper, scallions, bread crumbs, basil, salt, and pepper to the corn kernels in the bowl. Mix together, then shape into 4 equal-size burgers. Cover and let chill for 1 hour.

3 Move the grill rack up to reduce the heat, brush grill and burgers very lightly with a little oil. Then brush 1 teaspoon of maple syrup over each burger and cook again over medium heat for 4 minutes. Turn the burgers over very carefully to avoid them crumbling and cook for an additional 4–5 minutes, or until the burgers are cooked through. Pour over the remaining maple syrup and serve.

drumsticks in a piquant dressing

SERVES	PREP	+20	COOK
6	**10** mins	**mins** cooling	**2** hrs

This tasty dressing gives the chicken drumsticks a rich color as well as a fabulous flavor, which makes them irresistibly appetizing.

1 Preheat the barbecue. To make the dressing, place all the ingredients in a heavy-based pan and bring to a boil over low heat. Cover and let simmer gently for 1 hour, or until the onion and celery are very tender. Remove the pan from the heat and let cool.

2 Transfer the dressing to a food processor and process to a purée. Using a metal spoon, gently rub the purée through a fine-meshed strainer into a clean pan and bring to a boil over low heat. Let simmer gently for 25 minutes, or until reduced and thickened.

3 Brush the drumsticks with the sauce and cook over medium hot coals, turning and brushing with the sauce frequently, for 25–30 minutes. Serve. If you wish to serve the remaining sauce with the drumsticks, make sure that it is returned to boiling point first.

ingredients

12 chicken drumsticks

dressing
1 onion, minced
1 celery stalk, minced
1 garlic clove, minced
1 lb 12 oz/800 g canned
  minced tomatoes
3 tbsp brown sugar
1 tbsp paprika
$^{1}/_{4}$ tsp Tabasco sauce
1 tbsp Worcestershire sauce
pepper

ingredients

3 skinless, boneless chicken breasts
6 tbsp olive oil
4 tbsp lemon juice
$1/2$ small onion, grated
1 tbsp chopped fresh sage
8 tbsp sage and onion stuffing mix
6 tbsp boiling water
2 green bell peppers, seeded
corn oil, for oiling

sauce
1 tbsp olive oil
1 red bell pepper, seeded and
  finely chopped
1 small onion, finely chopped
pinch of sugar
$7^{1}/2$ oz/210 g canned chopped
  tomatoes

chicken skewers with bell pepper sauce

SERVES	PREP		COOK
4	15 mins	+1hr marinating/ chilling	35 mins

These kabobs are rather special and are well worth the extra effort needed to prepare them.

1 Cut the chicken into even-size pieces.

2 Mix the olive oil, lemon juice, grated onion, and sage together and pour the mixture into a plastic bag. Add the chicken, seal the bag, and shake to coat the chicken. Let marinate for at least 30 minutes, shaking the bag occasionally.

3 Place the stuffing mix in a small bowl, add the boiling water and mix well. Using a sharp knife, cut each bell pepper into 6 strips, then blanch them in boiling water for 3–4 minutes, or until softened. Drain and refresh under cold running water, then drain again. Form 1 teaspoon of the stuffing mixture into a ball and roll it up in a strip of bell pepper. Repeat for the remaining stuffing mixture and bell pepper strips. Thread the bell pepper rolls on to several metal skewers alternately with pieces of chicken. Let chill in the refrigerator until required.

4 Preheat the barbecue. To make the sauce, heat the olive oil in a small pan. Add the red bell pepper and onion and cook for 5 minutes. Add the sugar and tomatoes and simmer for 5 minutes. Keep warm.

5 Cook the skewers on an oiled rack over hot coals, basting frequently with the remaining marinade, for 15 minutes, or until the chicken is cooked. Serve with the red bell pepper sauce.

115

sesame chicken brochettes with cranberry sauce

MAKES	PREP		COOK
8	**15** mins	**+30 mins** chilling	**20-22** mins

The cranberries give the sauce a lovely tart flavor. It can be served hot or cold.

1 Cut the chicken into 1-inch pieces. Stir together the wine, sugar, oil, and salt and pepper to taste in a large bowl. Add the chicken and toss to coat. Marinate in the refrigerator for at least 30 minutes, turning the chicken occasionally.

2 To make the sauce, place the ingredients in a small saucepan and bring slowly to a boil, stirring. Simmer gently for 5–10 minutes, until the cranberries are soft. Taste and add extra sugar if desired. Keep warm or chill, as required.

3 Remove the chicken pieces from the marinade with a slotted spoon. Thread the chicken pieces onto 8 skewers, spacing them slightly apart to ensure even cooking.

4 Broil on an oiled rack over hot coals for 4–5 minutes on each side, until just cooked. Brush several times with the marinade during cooking.

5 Remove the chicken skewers from the rack and roll in the sesame seeds. Return to the barbecue and cook for about 1 minute on each side or until the sesame seeds are toasted. Serve with the cranberry sauce, new potatoes, and salad greens.

ingredients

4 skinless, boneless chicken breasts
4 tbsp dry white wine
1 tbsp light muscovado sugar
2 tbsp sunflower oil
$6^1/_2$ tbsp sesame seeds
salt and pepper

to serve
boiled new potatoes
salad greens

sauce
$1^1/_2$ cups cranberries
$^2/_3$ cup cranberry juice drink
2 tbsp light muscovado sugar

spicy chicken wings

SERVES	PREP		COOK
4	15 mins	+8hrs marinating	18-20 mins

ingredients

16 chicken wings
4 tbsp corn oil
4 tbsp light soy sauce
2-inch/5-cm piece of fresh
  gingerroot, coarsely chopped
2 garlic cloves, coarsely chopped
juice and grated rind of 1 lemon
2 tsp ground cinnamon
2 tsp ground turmeric
4 tbsp honey
salt and pepper

sauce
2 orange bell peppers
2 yellow bell peppers
corn oil, for brushing
1/2 cup plain yogurt
2 tbsp dark soy sauce
2 tbsp chopped fresh cilantro

Coated in a spicy marinade and served with a colorful, chargrilled bell pepper sauce, these delicious chicken wings are perfect as part of a summer barbecue lunch party.

1 Place the chicken wings in a large, shallow, nonmetallic dish. Put the oil, soy sauce, ginger, garlic, lemon rind and juice, cinnamon, turmeric, and honey into a food processor and process to a smooth purée. Season to taste with salt and pepper. Spoon the mixture over the chicken wings and turn until thoroughly coated, cover with plastic wrap and let marinate in the refrigerator for up to 8 hours.

2 Preheat the barbecue. To make the sauce, brush the bell peppers with the oil and cook over hot coals, turning frequently, for 10 minutes, or until the skin is blackened and charred. Remove from the barbecue and let cool slightly, then remove the skins and discard the seeds. Put the flesh into a food processor with the yogurt and process to a smooth purée. Transfer to a bowl and stir in the soy sauce and chopped cilantro.

3 Drain the chicken wings, reserving the marinade. Cook over medium hot coals, turning and brushing frequently with the reserved marinade, for 8–10 minutes, or until thoroughly cooked. Serve immediately with the sauce.

duck breasts with caesar salad

SERVES	PREP		COOK
6	**15** mins	**+12hrs** marinating	**15** mins

This is a marriage made in heaven—the richness of the duck is complemented by the refreshing salad.

1 Put the coriander seeds, juniper berries, peppercorns, and bay leaves into a mortar and add $^1/_2$ tsp salt. Grind to a powder. Rub the duck breasts all over with the spice mixture. Place in a dish, cover, and let marinate in the refrigerator overnight.

2 An hour before you are ready to cook, remove the duck from the refrigerator, and wipe off most of the spice mix with paper towels. Whisk together the orange juice and olive oil in a small bowl and set aside.

3 Meanwhile, prepare the salad. Put the anchovies, lemon juice, garlic, mustard, and egg yolk in a blender or food processor and process until smooth. With the machine running, gradually trickle in the olive oil until the dressing emulsifies. Season to taste. Place the lettuce in a bowl, add half the dressing, and 3 tbsp of the Parmesan. Toss well.

4 Brush the duck breasts with the orange juice mixture and grill, skin-side down, for 5 minutes. Turn, brush with more juice mixture and grill for 10–12 minutes, or until cooked to your liking. Let rest for 2–3 minutes, then slice into strips.

5 Divide the lettuce between 6 plates, sprinkle with the bread cubes, and top with the duck. Drizzle over the remaining dressing, sprinkle with the remaining Parmesan, and serve.

ingredients

1 tbsp coriander seeds
10 juniper berries
1 tsp green peppercorns
6 dried bay leaves, crumbled
1 lb 2 oz/500 g boneless duck breasts
1 tbsp orange juice
1 tbsp olive oil
salt and pepper

caesar salad

4 canned anchovies, chopped
6 tbsp lemon juice
2 garlic cloves, chopped
2 tsp Dijon mustard
1 large egg yolk
1$^1/_4$ cups olive oil
1 large romaine lettuce, torn into pieces
4 tbsp freshly grated Parmesan cheese
4 slices of bread, cubed and cooked until crisp

ingredients

marinade
1 red chili and 1 green chili,
  seeded and finely chopped
2 garlic cloves, chopped
$1^3/_4$ oz/50 g chopped fresh cilantro
1 tbsp finely chopped fresh lemongrass
$^1/_2$ tsp ground turmeric
$^1/_2$ tsp garam masala
2 tsp brown sugar
2 tbsp fish sauce
1 tbsp lime juice
salt and pepper

chicken
4 skinless, boneless chicken
  breasts, cut into small chunks

to garnish
chopped fresh cilantro

to serve
freshly cooked jasmine rice

thai-style chicken chunks

SERVES	PREP	+2$^1/_2$	COOK
4	**10** mins	**hrs** marinating	**20** mins

Ensure that you marinate the chicken for at least $2^1/_2$ hours to bring out the variety of fantastic flavors.

1 Put the red and green chilies, garlic, cilantro, and lemongrass into a food processor and process until coarsely chopped. Add the turmeric, garam masala, sugar, fish sauce, and lime juice, season well, and blend until smooth.

2 Put the chicken chunks into a nonmetallic (glass or ceramic) bowl, which will not react with acid. Pour over enough marinade to cover the chicken, then cover with plastic wrap and refrigerate for at least $2^1/_2$ hours. Cover the remaining marinade with plastic wrap and refrigerate until the chicken is ready.

3 When the chicken chunks are thoroughly marinated, lift them out and grill them over hot coals for 20 minutes or until cooked right through, turning them frequently and basting with the remaining marinade. Arrange the chicken on serving plates with some freshly cooked jasmine rice, garnish with chopped cilantro, and serve.

shrimpskewersfreshfishscrumptious
tunaburger...

fish &
seafood

shrimp with citrus salsa

SERVES	PREP	COOK
6	**25** mins	**6** mins

A fruity, herby salsa brings out the flavor of grilled shrimp. It can be prepared in advance of the barbecue, then left in the refrigerator to chill until your guests are ready to eat.

1 Preheat the barbecue. To make the salsa, peel the orange and cut into segments. Set aside any juice. Put the orange segments, apple quarters, chilies, garlic, cilantro, and mint into a food processor and process until smooth. With the motor running, add the lime juice through the feeder tube. Transfer the salsa to a serving bowl and season to taste with salt and pepper. Cover with plastic wrap and let chill in the refrigerator until required.

2 Using a sharp knife, remove and discard the heads from the shrimp, then remove the shells. Cut along the back of the shrimp and remove the dark intestinal vein. Rinse the shrimp under cold running water and pat dry with paper towels. Mix the chopped cilantro, cayenne, and corn oil together in a dish. Add the shrimp and toss well to coat.

3 Cook the shrimp over medium hot coals for 3 minutes on each side, or until they have changed color. Transfer to a large serving plate, garnish with fresh cilantro leaves, and serve immediately with lime wedges and the salsa.

ingredients

36 large, raw jumbo shrimp
2 tbsp finely chopped fresh
 cilantro
pinch of cayenne pepper
3–4 tbsp corn oil

to garnish
fresh cilantro leaves

to serve
lime wedges

salsa
1 orange
1 tart eating apple, peeled,
 quartered, and cored
2 fresh red chilies, seeded
 and chopped
1 garlic clove, chopped
8 fresh cilantro sprigs
8 fresh mint sprigs
4 tbsp lime juice
salt and pepper

smoky trout burgers with pesto relish

SERVES	PREP		COOK
4	**10** mins	**+1hr** chilling	**25-30** mins

Smoked fish and bacon work really well together here, especially when teamed with the fresh and fragrant pesto relish.

1 Cook the potatoes in a pan of lightly salted water for 15–20 minutes, or until cooked. Drain, mash, and place in a large bowl. Add the trout, horseradish, scallions, zucchini, and salt and pepper to taste. Mix together and shape into 4 equal-size burgers. Let chill for 1 hour, then coat in the flour and wrap each in 2 slices of bacon.

2 Meanwhile, prepare the relish. Place the basil, pine nuts, and garlic in a food processor and blend for 1 minute. With the motor running, gradually pour in the oil and continue to blend until all the oil has been incorporated. Scrape into a bowl and stir in the cheese, cucumber, scallions, and tomatoes. Spoon into a serving bowl.

3 Preheat the barbecue. Lightly brush the burgers with oil and then cook over medium hot coals for 3-4 minutes on each side until golden and piping hot. Serve.

ingredients

8 oz/225 g potatoes, cut into
 chunks
salt and pepper
12 oz/350 g smoked trout
 fillets, flaked
2 tsp creamed horseradish
6 scallions, finely chopped
6 oz/175 g zucchini, coarsely
 grated
2 tbsp whole-wheat flour
8 lean Canadian bacon slices
2 tbsp corn oil

pesto relish
3 tbsp fresh basil
generous $^1/_4$ cup pine nuts, toasted
3 garlic cloves
$^2/_3$ cup virgin olive oil
$1^1/_2$ oz/40 g Parmesan cheese,
 freshly grated
$1^1/_2$-inch/4-cm piece cucumber,
 peeled and finely diced
4 scallions, finely chopped
2 plum tomatoes, finely diced

nut-crusted halibut

SERVES	PREP	COOK
4	**5** mins	**10** mins

This dish is sure to impress and is so easy you'll be amazed. You can also cook the halibut in a ridged skillet if you can't get to the barbecue.

1 Brush the melted butter over the fish fillet.

2 Roll the fish in the chopped nuts, pressing down gently.

3 Preheat the barbecue. Cook the halibut over hot coals for about 10 minutes, turning once. Cooking time will depend on the thickness of the fillet, but the fish should be opaque, firm, and tender when done.

4 Remove the fish carefully from the rack to avoid it breaking up. Transfer to a large serving plate. Serve immediately.

ingredients

3 tbsp butter, melted
1 lb 10 oz/750 g halibut fillet
$^1/_2$ cup pistachio nuts, shelled
   and chopped very finely

barbecued trout

SERVES	PREP	COOK
4	15 mins	10 mins

Rainbow trout occasionally needs something extra to perk up its flavor. Try it cooked this way.

1 Rinse the trout inside and out under cold running water and thoroughly pat dry with paper towels.

2 Mix together the crushed chilies, paprika, and salt in a small bowl. Sprinkle half this mixture inside the cavities of the fish and divide the chopped shallots between them.

3 Brush the outsides of the fish with oil, then sprinkle with a little more of the spices. Grill on a medium barbecue, brushing occasionally with more oil and sprinkling with the remaining spices, for 4–5 minutes on each side, or until the fish is cooked through and the flesh flakes easily. Serve at once, garnished with lime wedges.

ingredients

4 rainbow trout, about 8–10 oz/
   225–280 g each, cleaned and
   heads removed
$1/2$ tsp crushed chilies
1 tbsp sweet paprika
1 tsp salt
4 small shallots, finely chopped
chili oil, for brushing

to garnish
lime wedges

ingredients

4 salmon steaks, about 6 oz/
  175 g each
¹/₂ lemon, sliced
1 onion, sliced into rings
4 fresh dill sprigs
4 canned artichoke hearts, drained
4 tbsp olive oil
4 tbsp chopped fresh flatleaf
  parsley
salt and pepper

salmon and artichoke packages

SERVES	PREP	COOK
4	15 mins	15 mins

Wrapping fish in a package before cooking it on the barbecue keeps it marvelously succulent.

1 Cut out 4 squares of foil, each large enough to enclose a fish steak. Place the salmon on the foil and top with the lemon slices, onion rings, and dill sprigs. Place an artichoke heart on each salmon steak.

2 Fold up the sides of the foil. Sprinkle 1 tablespoon olive oil and 1 tablespoon parsley into each package and season with a little salt and pepper. Fold over the edges of the foil securely.

3 Cook the packages on a medium barbecue for 15 minutes, turning once. Transfer to serving plates, open the tops of the packages and serve at once.

131

salmon teriyaki

SERVES	PREP		COOK
4	**10** mins	**+2hrs** marinating	**10** mins

This sweet but piquant Japanese-style teriyaki sauce complements the richness of salmon superbly. Choose some really crisp salad greens, such as romaine or iceberg, to serve with the warm sauce.

ingredients

4 salmon fillets, about 6 oz/
   175 g each

sauce
1 tbsp cornstarch
$^1/_2$ cup dark soy sauce
4 tbsp mirin or medium-dry
   sherry
2 tbsp rice or cider vinegar
2 tbsp honey

to serve
$^1/_2$ cucumber
mixed salad greens, torn into
   pieces
4 scallions, thinly sliced
   diagonally

1 Rinse the salmon fillets under cold running water, pat dry with paper towels, and place in a large, shallow, nonmetallic dish. To make the sauce, mix the cornstarch and soy sauce in a measuring cup until a paste forms, then stir in the remaining ingredients. Pour three-quarters of the sauce over the salmon, turning to coat. Cover with plastic wrap and let marinate in the refrigerator for 2 hours.

2 Preheat the barbecue. Cut the cucumber into thin sticks, then arrange the salad greens, cucumber, and scallions on 4 serving plates. Pour the remaining sauce into a pan and set over the barbecue to warm through.

3 Remove the salmon fillets from the dish and set aside the marinade. Cook the salmon over medium hot coals, brushing frequently with the reserved marinade, for 3–4 minutes on each side. Transfer the salmon fillets to the prepared serving plates and pour the warmed sauce over them. Serve immediately.

tasty thai fish patties

SERVES	PREP		COOK
4	10 mins	+30 mins chilling	5 mins

Bring the world of Thai food to your barbecue with these tasty patties. Serve with a good chili or soy sauce.

1 Cut the fish into large pieces, place in a food processor with the onion and chili (if using), and chop finely. Transfer the fish mixture to a mixing bowl and add all the other recipe ingredients. Mix well. The mixture should be quite thick and stiff.

2 Cover the bowl with plastic wrap and refrigerate for at least 30 minutes. Remove the fish from the refrigerator and mix once more.

3 Preheat the barbecue. Form small patties from the fish mixture, place on a hot barbecue, and cook in batches for 3–4 minutes, or until golden, turning once. If necessary, brush the rack with another tablespoon of oil before cooking the next batch of patties.

4 Transfer the cooked patties to a serving dish and garnish with cilantro leaves and stalks of lemongrass. Serve warm or cold, accompanied by chili sauce or sweet soy sauce.

ingredients

2 lb 4 oz/1 kg cod, haddock, whiting, or coley fillet, skinned, or a mixture
1 small onion
1 small fresh chili, deseeded (optional)
6–8 tbsp fresh bread crumbs
1 egg
2 tbsp fish sauce
juice of $1/2$ lime
1 tbsp finely chopped fresh lemongrass
2 tsp finely grated fresh ginger
2 tsp chopped fresh cilantro
pinch of sugar
pinch of salt
1–2 tbsp vegetable oil, for brushing

to garnish
fresh cilantro and lemongrass

to serve
chili sauce or sweet soy sauce

spanish shrimp

SERVES	PREP	COOK
6	**20** mins	**25** mins

These fresh shrimp are served with a fiery tomato and chili sauce. If you prefer a milder flavor, you can reduce the number of chilies.

1 Preheat the barbecue. Chop enough parsley to fill 2 tablespoons and set aside. To make the sauce, seed and chop the chilies, then put into a food processor with the onion and garlic and process until finely chopped. Add the tomatoes and olive oil and process to a purée.

2 Transfer the mixture to a pan set over very low heat, stir in the sugar and season to taste with salt and pepper. Let simmer very gently, without boiling, for 15 minutes. Transfer the sauce to an earthenware bowl and place on the side of the barbecue to keep warm.

3 Rinse the shrimp under cold running water and pat dry on paper towels. Mix the parsley and olive oil in a dish, add the shrimp, and toss well to coat. Cook the shrimp over medium hot coals for 3 minutes on each side, or until they have changed color. Transfer to a plate, garnish with lemon wedges, and serve with the sauce.

ingredients

1 bunch of fresh flat-leaf parsley
36 large, raw shrimp, shelled and
  deveined, tails left on
3–4 tbsp olive oil

to garnish
lemon wedges

sauce
6 fresh red chilies
1 onion, chopped
2 garlic cloves, chopped
1 lb 2 oz/500 g tomatoes, chopped
3 tbsp olive oil
pinch of sugar
salt and pepper

ingredients

1 lb/450 g angler fish tail
2 zucchinis
1 lemon
12 cherry tomatoes
8 bay leaves
4 tbsp olive oil
2 tbsp lemon juice
1 tsp chopped fresh thyme
$^1/_2$ tsp lemon pepper
salt

to serve
salad greens
fresh crusty bread

angler fish skewers with zucchinis & lemon

SERVES **4**

PREP **10** mins

COOK **20** mins

A simple basting sauce is brushed over these tasty kabobs, which make a perfect light meal served with bread and salad.

1 Preheat the barbecue. Using a sharp knife, cut the fish into 2-inch/5-cm chunks. Cut the zucchinis into thick slices and the lemon into wedges.

2 Thread the angler fish, zucchinis, lemon, tomatoes, and bay leaves on to 4 metal skewers.

3 Mix the olive oil, lemon juice, thyme, lemon pepper, and salt to taste together in a small bowl, then brush liberally all over the fish, lemon, tomatoes, and bay leaves on the skewers.

4 Cook the skewers over medium hot coals for 15 minutes, basting frequently with the remaining oil mixture. Serve the skewers with salad greens and plenty of fresh crusty bread.

fresh tuna burgers with mango salsa

SERVES	PREP		COOK
4-6	**15** mins	**+1hr** chilling	**23-32** mins

Tuna is best eaten slightly pink as it can be rather dry if overcooked. It is also important that the burgers are piping hot before serving.

1 Cook the sweet potatoes in a pan of lightly salted boiling water for 15–20 minutes, or until tender. Drain well, then mash and place in a food processor. Cut the tuna into chunks and add to the potatoes.

2 Add the scallions, zucchini, chili, and mango chutney to the food processor and, using the pulse button, blend together. Shape into 4–6 equal-size burgers, then cover and let chill for 1 hour.

3 Meanwhile make the salsa. Slice the mango flesh, reserving 8 good slices for serving. Finely chop the remainder, then mix with the tomatoes, chili, cucumber, cilantro, and honey. Mix well, then spoon into a small bowl. Cover and let stand for 30 minutes to allow the flavors to develop.

4 Preheat the barbecue. When hot, add the burgers and cook over hot coals for 4–6 minutes on each side or until piping hot. Serve.

ingredients

8 oz/225 g sweet potatoes, chopped
salt
1 lb/450 g fresh tuna steaks
6 scallions, finely chopped
6 oz/175 g zucchini, grated
1 fresh red jalapeño chili, seeded and finely chopped
2 tbsp prepared mango chutney
1 tbsp corn oil

mango salsa

1 large ripe mango, peeled and seeded
2 ripe tomatoes, finely chopped
1 fresh red jalapeño chili, seeded and finely chopped
$1^1/_2$-inch/4-cm piece cucumber, finely diced
1 tbsp chopped fresh cilantro
1–2 tsp honey

fish burgers

SERVES	PREP		COOK
4	**15** mins	**+1hr** chilling	**23–30** mins

These burgers have a wonderful subtle smoky flavor due to the addition of smoked haddock.

1 Cook the potatoes in a pan of lightly salted boiling water for 15–20 minutes, or until tender. Drain well and mash. Chop the fish into small pieces, then place in a food processor with the mashed potatoes, lemon rind, parsley, and salt and pepper to taste. Using the pulse button, blend together. Shape into 4 equal-size burgers and coat in the flour. Cover and let chill for 30 minutes.

2 Place the egg and bread crumbs in 2 separate bowls and coat the burgers first in the egg, allowing any excess to drip back into the bowl, then in the bread crumbs. Let chill for an additional 30 minutes.

3 Preheat the barbecue. When hot, add the burgers and cook over hot coals for 4–5 minutes on each side or until golden and cooked through. Serve.

ingredients

5 oz/140 g potatoes, cut into chunks
salt and pepper
8 oz/225 g cod fillet, skinned
8 oz/225 g smoked haddock, skinned
1 tbsp grated lemon rind

1 tbsp chopped fresh parsley
1–2 tbsp all-purpose flour
1 egg, beaten
$1^1/_2$ cups fresh white bread crumbs
2 tbsp corn oil

shrimp & bell pepper kabobs

SERVES
4

PREP
15
mins

+3-4 hrs
marinating

COOK
4-5
mins

ingredients

marinade
2 scallions, trimmed and chopped
2 garlic cloves, finely chopped
1 green chili and 1 small red chili, seeded and finely chopped
1 tbsp grated fresh gingerroot
1 tbsp chopped fresh chives
4 tbsp lime juice
1 tbsp finely grated lime zest
2 tbsp chili oil
salt and pepper

kabobs
24 jumbo shrimp, peeled and deveined, but with tails left on
2 bell peppers, 1 red and 1 green, seeded and cut into small chunks

to garnish
wedges of lime

to serve
freshly cooked rice or Napa cabbage

Zesty and with a bit of a kick, these kabobs are sure to jazz up your barbecue.

1 Put the scallions, garlic, chilies, ginger, chives, lime juice, lime zest, and chili oil into a food processor and season well with salt and pepper. Process until smooth, then transfer to a nonmetallic (glass or ceramic) bowl, which will not react with acid.

2 Thread the shrimp onto skewers, alternating them with the red and green bell pepper chunks. When the skewers are full (leave a small space at either end), transfer them to the bowl and turn them in the mixture until they are well coated. Cover with plastic wrap and place in the refrigerator to marinate for 3–4 hours.

3 Grill the kabobs over hot coals for 4–5 minutes or until the shrimp are cooked right through (but do not overcook), turning them frequently and basting with the remaining marinade. Arrange the skewers on a bed of rice or Napa cabbage, garnish with lime wedges and chopped fresh chives, and serve.

chargrilled tuna with chili salsa

SERVES	PREP		COOK
4	**15** mins	**+1hr** marinating	**20** mins

A firm fish such as tuna is an excellent choice for barbecues, as it is quite meaty and doesn't break up during cooking. Here it is served with a colorful and spicy chili salsa.

1 Rinse the tuna thoroughly under cold running water and pat dry with paper towels, then place in a large, shallow, nonmetallic dish. Sprinkle the lime rind and juice and the olive oil over the fish. Season to taste with salt and pepper, cover with plastic wrap, and let marinate in the refrigerator for up to 1 hour.

2 Preheat the barbecue. To make the salsa, brush the bell peppers with the olive oil and cook over hot coals, turning frequently, for 10 minutes, or until the skin is blackened and charred. Remove from the barbecue and let cool slightly, then remove the skins and discard the seeds. Put the bell peppers into a food processor with the remaining salsa ingredients and process to a purée. Transfer to a bowl and season to taste with salt and pepper.

3 Cook the tuna over hot coals for 4–5 minutes on each side, until golden. Transfer to serving plates, garnish with cilantro sprigs, and serve with the salsa.

ingredients

4 tuna steaks, about 6 oz/
  175 g each
grated rind and juice of 1 lime
2 tbsp olive oil
salt and pepper

to garnish
fresh cilantro sprigs

chili salsa
2 orange bell peppers
1 tbsp olive oil
juice of 1 lime
juice of 1 orange
2–3 fresh red chilies, seeded
  and chopped
pinch of cayenne pepper

asian shrimp skewers

SERVES	PREP		COOK
4	15 mins	+2hrs marinating	4-5 mins

ingredients

marinade
scant $1/2$ cup vegetable oil
2 tbsp chili oil
scant $1/4$ cup lemon juice
1 tbsp rice wine or sherry
2 scallions, trimmed and
  finely chopped
2 garlic cloves, finely chopped
1 tbsp grated fresh gingerroot
1 tbsp chopped fresh lemongrass
2 tbsp chopped fresh cilantro
salt and pepper

skewers
2 lb 4 oz/1 kg jumbo shrimp,
  peeled and deveined, but with
  tails left on

to garnish
wedges of lemon
chopped fresh chives

to serve
freshly cooked jasmine rice

These shrimp skewers are so easy and add a touch of the exotic to your barbecue platter.

1 Put the oils, lemon juice, rice wine, scallions, garlic, ginger, lemongrass, and cilantro into a food processor and season well with salt and pepper. Process until smooth, then transfer to a nonmetallic (glass or ceramic) bowl, which will not react with acid.

2 Add the shrimp to the bowl and turn them in the mixture until they are well coated. Cover with plastic wrap and place in the refrigerator to marinate for at least 2 hours.

3 When the shrimp are thoroughly marinated, lift them out and thread them onto skewers leaving a small space at either end. Grill them over hot coals for 4–5 minutes or until cooked right through (but do not overcook), turning them frequently and basting with the remaining marinade. Arrange the skewers on a bed of freshly cooked jasmine rice, garnish with lemon wedges and chopped fresh chives, and serve.

caribbean sea bass

SERVES	PREP	COOK
6	**15** mins	**20** mins

A fish basket is essential, as it is almost impossible to turn the fish without breaking it up and spoiling its spectacular appearance.

1 Preheat the barbecue. Rinse the sea bass inside and out under cold running water, then pat dry with paper towels. Using a sharp knife, make a series of shallow diagonal slashes along each side of the fish. Brush each slash with a little olive oil, then sprinkle over the saffron powder.

2 Brush a large fish basket with olive oil and place the fish in the basket, but do not close it. Season the cavity with salt and pepper. Place the lemon and lime slices and the thyme in the cavity without overfilling it.

3 Close the basket and cook the fish over medium hot coals for 10 minutes on each side. Carefully transfer to a large serving plate, garnish with lemon and lime slices, and serve immediately.

ingredients

3 lb 5 oz/1.5 kg sea bass, cleaned and scaled
1–2 tsp olive oil
1 tsp saffron powder
salt and pepper
$^{1}/_{2}$ lemon, sliced, plus extra to garnish
1 lime, sliced, plus extra to garnish
1 bunch of fresh thyme

ingredients

2 porgy, about 12 oz/350 g each,
  cleaned and scaled

marinade
6 tbsp olive oil
2 tbsp white wine or dry sherry
2 garlic cloves, finely chopped
2 bay leaves, crumbled
1 tbsp fresh thyme leaves
1 tbsp snipped fresh chives
salt and pepper
12–16 large grape leaves

to garnish
thyme leaves
half a grilled lemon

porgy wrapped in grape leaves

SERVES	PREP		COOK
4	10-15 mins	1hr marinating +20mins soaking	15 mins

Grape leaves protect the delicate flesh of porgy during cooking as well as imparting a subtle flavor.

1 Rinse the fish and pat dry with paper towels. Score both fish 2–3 times diagonally on each side and place in a large dish. Mix together the olive oil, white wine, garlic, bay leaves, thyme, and chives in a small bowl and season with salt and pepper. Spoon the mixture over the fish, turning to coat. Cover and let marinate for 1 hour.

2 If using grape leaves preserved in brine, soak them in hot water for 20 minutes, then rinse well and pat dry. If using fresh grape leaves, blanch in boiling water for 3 minutes, then refresh under cold water, drain, and pat dry.

3 Drain the fish, reserving the marinade. Wrap each fish in grape leaves to enclose. Brush with the marinade. Grill on a medium barbecue for 6 minutes on each side, brushing with more marinade occasionally.

crunch!vegetarianburgermouthwatering
crispsaladstuffedtortillas...

vegetables

yam and red bell pepper burgers

SERVES	PREP		COOK
4-6	**10** mins	**+1hr** chilling	**25-32** mins

If you prefer them to be chunkier, blend the mixture only briefly and do not peel the bell peppers.

1 Cook the yam in a pan of lightly salted boiling water for 15–20 minutes, or until tender. Drain well and place in a food processor.

2 Add the chickpeas, red bell peppers, garlic, olives, sesame seeds, cilantro, and salt and pepper to the yam in the food processor and, using the pulse button, blend together. Shape into 4–6 equal-size burgers, then coat in the flour. Cover and let chill for 1 hour.

3 Preheat the barbecue. When hot, add the burgers and cook over hot coals for 5–6 minutes on each side or until cooked and piping hot. Serve.

ingredients

8 oz/225 g yam, peeled and cut into chunks
salt and pepper
14 oz/400 g canned chickpeas, drained
2 red bell peppers, seeded and peeled
2–3 garlic cloves, crushed
$1/2$ cup pitted black olives
2 tbsp sesame seeds
1 tbsp chopped fresh cilantro
2 tbsp whole-wheat flour
2 tbsp corn oil

corn with blue cheese dressing

SERVES	PREP	COOK
6	**15** mins	**15–20** mins

Cook the corn cobs as soon after purchase as possible because they quickly lose their sweetness.

ingredients

5 oz/140 g Danablu cheese
5 oz/140 g curd cheese
$^1/_2$ cup strained plain yogurt
salt and pepper
6 corn ears in their husks

1 Preheat the barbecue. Crumble the Danablu cheese, then place in a bowl. Beat with a wooden spoon until creamy. Beat in the curd cheese until thoroughly blended. Gradually beat in the yogurt and season to taste with salt and pepper. Cover with plastic wrap and let chill in the refrigerator until required.

2 Fold back the husks on each corn and remove the silks. Smooth the husks back into place. Cut out 6 rectangles of foil, each large enough to enclose a corn. Wrap the corn in the foil.

3 Cook the corn over hot coals, turning frequently, for 15–20 minutes. Unwrap the corn and discard the foil. Peel back the husk on one side of each and trim off with a sharp knife or kitchen scissors. Serve immediately with the blue cheese dressing.

spicy vegetarian sausages

SERVES
4

PREP
15
mins

+45 mins
chilling

COOK
15
mins

Vegetarian sausages are no longer the poor relation with a recipe full of flavor and inspiration.

1 Put the garlic, onion, chili, mashed kidney beans, bread crumbs, almonds, rice, and cheese into a large bowl. Stir in the egg yolk and oregano, then season with salt and plenty of pepper.

2 Using your hands, form the mixture into sausage shapes. Roll each sausage in a little flour, then transfer to a bowl, cover with plastic wrap, and refrigerate for 45 minutes.

3 Brush a piece of aluminum foil with oil, then put the sausages on the foil and brush them with a little more vegetable oil. Transfer the sausages and foil to the barbecue grill. Grill over hot coals, turning the sausages frequently, for about 15 minutes or until cooked right through. Serve with bread rolls, cooked sliced onion and tomato, and tomato catsup and/or mustard.

ingredients

1 garlic clove, finely chopped
1 onion, finely chopped
1 red chili, seeded and finely chopped
14 oz/400 g canned red kidney beans, rinsed, drained, and mashed
2 cups fresh bread crumbs
$^1/_3$ cup almonds, toasted and ground
1$^3/_4$ oz/50 g cooked rice
$^1/_2$ cup grated colby cheese
1 egg yolk
1 tbsp chopped fresh oregano
flour, for dusting
salt and pepper
vegetable oil, for brushing

to serve
fresh bread rolls
sliced onion, lightly cooked
sliced tomato, lightly cooked
tomato catsup and/or mustard

ingredients

12 oz/350 g firm tofu (drained
  weight)
1 red bell pepper
1 yellow bell pepper
2 zucchinis
8 white mushrooms

to garnish
carrot sticks
lemon slices

marinade
grated rind and juice of $^1/_2$ lemon
1 garlic clove, crushed
$^1/_2$ tsp chopped fresh rosemary
$^1/_2$ tsp chopped fresh thyme
1 tbsp walnut oil

marinated tofu skewers

SERVES	PREP	+20	COOK
4	20 mins	mins marinating	10-15 mins

Tofu is full of protein, vitamins, and minerals, and it develops a fabulous flavor when it is marinated in garlic and herbs.

1 To make the marinade, mix the lemon rind and juice, garlic, rosemary, thyme, and walnut oil together in a shallow dish. Drain the tofu, pat it dry on paper towels and cut it into squares. Add to the marinade and toss to coat. Let marinate for 20–30 minutes.

2 Preheat the barbecue. Seed the bell peppers and cut into 1-inch/2.5-cm pieces. Blanch in boiling water for 4 minutes, refresh in cold water, and drain. Using a canelle knife or potato peeler, remove strips of peel from the zucchinis. Cut the zucchinis into 1-inch/2.5-cm chunks.

3 Remove the tofu from the marinade, reserving the liquid for basting. Thread the tofu on to 8 presoaked wooden skewers, alternating with the bell peppers, zucchinis, and mushrooms.

4 Cook the skewers over medium hot coals for 6 minutes, turning and basting with the marinade. Transfer the skewers to warmed serving plates, garnish with carrot sticks and slices of lemon, and serve.

eggplants with minted yogurt dip

ingredients

1 cup unsweetened Greek yogurt
$^1/_2$ cucumber, diced
4 scallions, finely chopped
1 garlic clove, finely chopped
3 tbsp chopped fresh mint
salt and pepper
2 tbsp olive oil
2 eggplants, thinly sliced

SERVES	PREP	COOK
4	15 mins	10 mins

This makes a delicious appetizer for a barbecue party or can be served as part of a vegetarian barbecue meze.

1 First, make the dip. Dice the cucumber. Place the yogurt in a bowl and beat well until smooth. Stir in the cucumber, scallions, garlic, and mint. Season to taste with salt and pepper. Transfer to a serving bowl, cover with plastic wrap, and chill in the refrigerator.

2 Season the olive oil to taste with plenty of salt and pepper, then brush the eggplant slices generously with the seasoned oil.

3 Cook the eggplants on a hot barbecue for 5 minutes on each side, brushing with more oil, if necessary. Serve immediately with the minted yogurt dip.

vegetarian brochettes

SERVES	PREP	COOK
4	20 mins	8-10 mins

The great thing about tofu is its ability to absorb other flavors, in this case a mustard and honey flavored glaze.

ingredients

2 zucchinis
1 yellow bell pepper, seeded and quartered
8 oz/225 g firm tofu (drained weight)
4 cherry tomatoes
4 pearl onions
8 white mushrooms

honey glaze
2 tbsp olive oil
1 tbsp Meaux mustard
1 tbsp honey
salt and pepper

1 Preheat the barbecue. Using a vegetable peeler, peel off strips of skin along the length of the zucchinis to leave alternate yellow and green stripes, then cut each zucchini into 8 thick slices. Cut each of the yellow bell pepper quarters in half. Cut the drained tofu into 1-inch/2.5-cm cubes.

2 Thread the pieces of bell pepper, zucchini slices, tofu cubes, cherry tomatoes, pearl onions, and white mushrooms onto 4 metal skewers. To make the glaze, mix the olive oil, mustard, and honey together in a measuring cup and season to taste with salt and pepper.

3 Brush the brochettes with the honey glaze and cook over medium hot coals, turning and brushing frequently with the glaze, for 8–10 minutes. Serve.

stuffed tortillas

SERVES
4

PREP
10-15
mins

COOK
15-17
mins

Here is a barbecue dish with a difference. Delicious, unusual and best of all—vegetarian!

1 Cook the red bell peppers on the barbecue grill, skin side down, for about 5 minutes or until the skins are blackened and charred. Transfer them to a plastic bag, seal the bag, and set aside.

2 Grill the sausages over hot coals for 10–12 minutes or until cooked right through, turning them occasionally. While the sausages are cooking, put the kidney beans, tomatoes, onion, garlic, lime juice, and basil into a large bowl. Season with salt and pepper and mix until well combined.

3 Take the bell pepper quarters from the plastic bag and remove the skins. Chop the flesh into small pieces and add it to the kidney bean mixture. About one minute before the sausages are ready, warm the tortillas on the grill for a few seconds.

4 Remove the sausages from the grill and cut them into slices. Fill the tortillas with sausage slices, kidney bean salsa, shredded lettuce, tomato slices, and sour cream. Serve at once.

ingredients

2 red bell peppers, seeded and
  cut into quarters
4 vegetarian sausages
11^1/$_2$ oz/325 g canned red
  kidney beans, drained, rinsed,
  and drained again
4 large tomatoes, chopped
1 large onion, chopped
1 garlic clove, chopped
1 tbsp lime juice
1 tbsp chopped fresh basil
salt and pepper
4 large wheat or corn tortillas,
  or 8 small ones

to serve
shredded lettuce
slices of fresh tomato
sour cream

163

the ultimate vegetarian burger

SERVES 4-6	PREP 10-12 mins	+1hr chilling	COOK 30-32 mins

You can, if you like, substitute the flageolets (green kidney beans) for black-eye peas or red kidney beans.

1 Cook the rice in a pan of lightly salted boiling water for 20 minutes, or until tender. Drain and place in a food processor.

2 Add the beans, cashews, garlic, onion, corn, tomato paste, oregano, and salt and pepper to the rice in the food processor and, using the pulse button, blend together. Shape into 4–6 equal-size burgers, then coat in the flour. Cover and let chill for 1 hour.

3 Preheat the barbecue. When hot, add the burgers and cook over hot coals for 5–6 minutes on each side or until cooked and piping hot. Thickly slice the provolone (if using), and cook for 1-2 minutes each side or until slightly browned, but not too floppy. Assemble the burger with tomato and lettuce, if liked, and place the cheese on top of the burger. Serve.

ingredients

scant $^1/_2$ cup brown rice

salt and pepper

14 oz/400 g canned flageolets, drained

scant 1 cup unsalted cashews

3 garlic cloves

1 red onion, cut into wedges

$^1/_2$ cup corn kernels

2 tbsp tomato paste

1 tbsp chopped fresh oregano

2 tbsp whole-wheat flour

2 tbsp corn oil

provolone (optional)

tomato slices and lettuce (optional)

vegetable satay

SERVES	PREP		COOK
4	**10** mins	**+4hrs** marinating	**15** mins

Colorful vegetable kabobs are delightful served with a slightly crunchy peanut sauce.

1 Put the zucchini and eggplant chunks, corn cobs, and mushrooms in a bowl. Mix together the oil and lime juice in a pitcher and pour over the vegetables. Stir well, cover, and let marinate for 4 hours.

2 To make the satay sauce, pour the coconut milk into a small pan and stir in the peanut butter. Heat gently, stirring constantly, until smooth. Stir in the soy sauce, sugar, and the pinch of chili powder. Transfer to the side of the barbecue to keep warm.

3 Drain the vegetables, reserving the marinade, and thread them alternately onto 4 skewers. Grill on a medium barbecue, turning occasionally for about 10 minutes. Serve at once, with the satay sauce.

ingredients

marinade
3 zucchini, cut into 1-inch
  2.5-cm chunks
1 eggplant, cut into 1-inch/
  2.5-cm chunks
8 baby corn
8 white mushrooms
3 tbsp peanut oil
3 tbsp lime juice

satay sauce
$^3/_4$ cup canned coconut milk
scant $^1/_2$ cup crunchy
  peanut butter
2 tsp dark soy sauce
1 tsp brown sugar
pinch chili powder

vegetable platter

SERVES **4**

PREP **25** mins

+1hr marinating

COOK **30** mins

ingredients

2 red onions
2 white onions
2 fennel bulbs
6 baby corn
12 cherry tomatoes
4 tbsp olive oil
1 tbsp lemon juice
3 garlic cloves, finely chopped
2 tbsp chopped fresh marjoram
salt and pepper
1 green bell pepper
1 yellow bell pepper
1 orange bell pepper
1 red bell pepper
1 tbsp corn oil

to serve
mayonnaise

This cornucopia of chargrilled vegetables makes a wonderful vegetarian barbecue or accompaniment.

1 Using a sharp knife, cut the red and white onions in half and set aside until required. Blanch the fennel and baby corn in a large pan of boiling water for 2 minutes. Drain, refresh under cold running water and drain again. Cut the fennel bulbs in half and place in a large, shallow, nonmetallic dish. Cut the baby corn in half across the center and add to the dish with the tomatoes and onions.

2 Mix the oil, lemon juice, garlic, and marjoram in a measuring cup and season to taste with salt and pepper. Pour the mixture over the vegetables, cover, and let marinate for 1 hour.

3 Preheat the barbecue. Drain the vegetables, reserving the marinade. Thread the corn and cherry tomatoes alternately onto presoaked wooden skewers. Brush the bell peppers with oil and cook over medium hot coals, turning, for 10 minutes. Add the onion and fennel to the barbecue and cook, brushing with the marinade, for 5 minutes. Turn the onion and fennel and brush with marinade. Add the skewers, brush with marinade, and cook, turning and brushing frequently with more marinade, for 10 minutes. Transfer the vegetables to a large plate and serve with the mayonnaise.

stuffed tomato packages

SERVES	PREP		COOK
4	**15** mins	**+15 mins** cooling	**20** mins

An unusual filling for stuffed tomatoes, the spinach and cheese are given extra flavor with toasted sunflower seeds.

1 Preheat the barbecue. Heat the oil in a heavy-bottom pan. Add the sunflower seeds and cook, stirring constantly, for 2 minutes, or until golden. Add the onion and cook over low heat, stirring occasionally, for 5 minutes, or until softened but not browned. Add the garlic and spinach, cover, and cook for 2–3 minutes, or until the spinach has wilted. Remove the pan from the heat and season to taste with nutmeg, salt and pepper. Let cool.

2 Using a sharp knife, cut off and set aside a thin slice from the top of each tomato and scoop out the flesh with a teaspoon, taking care not to pierce the shell. Chop the flesh and stir it into the spinach mixture with the mozzarella cheese.

3 Fill the tomato shells with the spinach and cheese mixture and replace the tops. Cut 4 squares of foil, each large enough to enclose a tomato. Place one tomato in the center of each square and fold up the sides to enclose securely. Cook over hot coals, turning occasionally, for 10 minutes. Serve immediately in the packages.

ingredients

1 tbsp olive oil
2 tbsp sunflower seeds
1 onion, finely chopped
1 garlic clove, finely chopped
1 lb 2 oz/500 g fresh spinach, thick
  stalks removed and leaves shredded
pinch of freshly grated nutmeg
salt and pepper
4 beefsteak tomatoes
5 oz/140 g mozzarella cheese, diced

ingredients

1 corn ear
1 chayote, peeled and
 cut into chunks
1 ripe plantain, peeled and cut
 into thick slices
1 eggplant, cut into chunks
1 red bell pepper, seeded and
 cut into chunks
1 green bell pepper, seeded and
 cut into chunks
1 onion, cut into wedges
8 white mushrooms
4 cherry tomatoes

marinade
$^2/_3$ cup tomato juice
4 tbsp corn oil
4 tbsp lime juice
3 tbsp dark soy sauce
1 shallot, finely chopped
2 garlic cloves, finely chopped
1 fresh green chili, seeded and
 finely chopped
$^1/_2$ tsp ground cinnamon
pepper

spicy caribbean kabobs

SERVES	PREP		COOK
4	**20** mins	**+3hrs** marinating	**15** mins

Bring a taste of the tropics to your barbecue with a sizzling dish that is also suitable for vegans.

1 Using a sharp knife, remove the husks and silks from the corn and cut into 1-inch/2.5-cm thick slices. Blanch the chayote chunks in boiling water for 2 minutes. Drain, refresh under cold running water, and drain again. Place the chayote chunks in a large bowl with the corn slices and the remaining ingredients.

2 Mix all the marinade ingredients together in a measuring cup, seasoning to taste with pepper. Pour the marinade over the vegetables, tossing to coat. Cover with plastic wrap and let marinate in the refrigerator for 3 hours.

3 Preheat the barbecue. Drain the vegetables, reserving the marinade. Thread the vegetables onto several metal skewers. Cook over hot coals, turning and brushing frequently with the reserved marinade, for 10–15 minutes. Transfer to a large serving plate and serve immediately.

vegetarian chili burgers

SERVES	PREP		COOK
4-6	20 mins	+1hr chilling	24-28 mins

To maximize the cilantro's contribution, chop the root and stalks into the mixture as well as the leaves.

1 Cook the bulgur wheat in a pan of lightly salted water for 12 minutes, or until cooked. Drain and set aside.

2 Place the beans in a food processor with the chilies, garlic, scallions, pepper, cilantro, and half the cheese. Using the pulse button, chop finely. Add to the cooked bulgur wheat with salt and pepper to taste. Mix well, then shape into 4–6 equal-size burgers. Cover and let chill for 1 hour. Coat the burgers in the flour.

3 Preheat the barbecue. When hot, add the burgers and cook over hot coals for 5–6 minutes on each side or until piping hot.

4 Place 1–2 slices of tomato on top of each burger and sprinkle with the remaining cheese. Cook for 2–3 minutes, or until the cheese starts to melt. Serve.

ingredients

$1/2$ cup bulgur wheat
salt and pepper
$10^1/2$ oz/300 g canned red kidney beans, drained and rinsed
$10^1/2$ oz/300 g canned cannellini beans, drained
1–2 fresh red jalapeño chilies, seeded and coarsely chopped
2–3 garlic cloves
6 scallions, coarsely chopped
1 yellow bell pepper, seeded, peeled, and chopped
1 tbsp chopped fresh cilantro
4 oz/115 g mature Cheddar cheese, grated
2 tbsp whole-wheat flour
1–2 tbsp corn oil
1 large tomato, sliced

provolone cheese & vegetable kabobs

SERVES	PREP		COOK
4	10 mins	+2hrs marinating	5-10 mins

ingredients

marinade
4 tbsp extra-virgin olive oil
2 tbsp balsamic vinegar
2 garlic cloves, finely chopped
1 tbsp chopped fresh cilantro
salt and pepper

kabobs
8 oz/225 g provolone cheese
12 white mushrooms
8 pearl onions
12 cherry tomatoes
2 zucchini, cut into small
  chunks
1 red bell pepper, seeded and
  cut into small chunks

to garnish
chopped fresh cilantro

to serve
freshly cooked rice or fresh
  salad greens
fresh crusty bread

Provolone is just perfect for the barbecue and these kabobs are bursting with color and taste.

1 Put the oil, vinegar, garlic, and cilantro into a large bowl. Season with salt and pepper and mix until well combined.

2 Cut the provolone cheese into bite-size cubes. Thread the cubes onto skewers, alternating them with whole white mushrooms, pearl onions, cherry tomatoes, and zucchini and red bell pepper chunks. When the skewers are full (leave a small space at either end), transfer them to the bowl and turn them in the mixture until they are well coated. Cover with plastic wrap and place in the refrigerator to marinate for at least 2 hours.

3 When the skewers are thoroughly marinated, grill them over hot coals for 5–10 minutes or until they are cooked to your taste, turning them frequently and basting with the remaining marinade. Arrange the skewers on a bed of freshly cooked rice or fresh mixed salad greens, garnish with cilantro leaves, and serve with fresh crusty bread.

desserts

cinnamon fruit with chocolate sauce

SERVES 4 **PREP** 10 mins **COOK** 10 mins

Fresh fruit kebabs are coated with spicy butter before grilling and are then served with an easy to prepare, rich chocolate sauce.

1 Preheat the barbecue. To make the sauce, break the chocolate into pieces and melt with the butter in a pan over low heat. Stir in the sugar and evaporated milk and cook, stirring, until the sauce has thickened and smooth. Remove from the heat, pour into a bowl and set over a low part of the barbecue to keep hot.

2 Cut the pineapple slices into chunks. Thread the pineapple chunks, kiwifruit, and strawberries alternately onto the prepared wooden skewers. Mix the butter, cinnamon and orange juice together in a small bowl. Brush the fruit kebabs all over with the cinnamon butter.

3 Cook the kebabs over hot coals, turning and basting frequently with the remaining cinnamon butter, for 2–3 minutes, until golden. Just before serving, stir the vanilla extract into the chocolate sauce.

ingredients

¼ teaspoon ground cinnamon

9 oz/250 g semisweet chocolate

2 oz/25 g butter

⅓ cup superfine sugar

½ cup evaporated milk

1 teaspoon vanilla extract

totally tropical pineapple

SERVES	PREP	COOK
4	15 mins	6-8 mins

As this succulent dessert is cooking the delicious aroma of fresh pineapple will transport you to a Caribbean beach.

1 Preheat the barbecue. Using a sharp knife, cut off the crown of the pineapple, then cut the fruit into 3/4-inch/2-cm thick slices. Cut away the peel from each slice and flick out the "eyes" with the tip of the knife. Stamp out the cores with an apple corer or small cookie cutter.

2 Mix the rum, sugar, ginger, and butter together in a measuring cup, stirring constantly, until the sugar has dissolved. Brush the pineapple rings with the rum mixture.

3 Cook the pineapple rings over hot coals for 3–4 minutes on each side. Transfer to serving plates and serve immediately with the remaining rum mixture poured over them.

baked bananas

SERVES	PREP	COOK
4	**30** mins	**10** mins

ingredients

8 oz/225 g strawberries
2 tbsp superfine sugar
6 tbsp Marsala wine
¹/₂ tsp ground cinnamon
4 slices panettone
4 tbsp mascarpone cheese

panettone with mascarpone & strawberries

SERVES 4   **PREP 10 mins**   **+30 mins chilling**   **COOK 5 mins**

Panettone is a sweet Italian fruit bread. It is delicious toasted and topped with mascapone cheese and marinated strawberries.

1 Hull and slice the strawberries and place them in a bowl. Add the sugar, Marsala, and cinnamon to the strawberries.

2 Toss the strawberries in the sugar and cinnamon mixture until they are well coated. Let chill in the refrigerator for at least 30 minutes.

3 Preheat the barbecue. When ready to serve, transfer the slices of panettone to a rack set over medium hot coals. Cook the panettone for 1 minute on each side, or until golden brown.

4 Remove the panettone from the barbecue and transfer to serving plates. Top the panettone with the mascarpone cheese and the marinated strawberries. Serve immediately.

stuffed pears

SERVES
4

PREP
20
mins

COOK
20
mins

It is a popular practice to sprinkle strawberries with pepper to bring out their flavor—this is equally effective with other fruit.

1 Preheat the barbecue. Cut out 4 squares of foil, each large enough to enclose the pears, and grease with the butter. Halve and core the pears, but do not peel. Brush the cut surfaces with lemon juice. Place 2 pear halves on each of the foil squares, brush them with the rosehip syrup and sprinkle with the peppercorns.

2 Place the red currants in a bowl and sprinkle with the sugar. Spoon the red currant mixture into the cavities of the pears. Fold up the sides of the foil to enclose the pears securely.

3 Cook over hot coals for 20 minutes. Serve immediately with ice cream.

fruity skewers with chocolate dip

SERVES	PREP	COOK
4	20 mins	10-15 mins

1

2

special peach melba

SERVES
4

PREP
15 mins

+15 mins marinating

COOK
3-5 mins

The elegant simplicity of this rich, fruity dessert makes it the perfect end to a special occasion barbecue party.

1 Place the peach halves in a large, shallow dish and sprinkle with the brown sugar. Pour the amaretto liqueur over them, cover with plastic wrap and let marinate for 1 hour.

2 Meanwhile, using the back of a spoon, press the raspberries through a fine strainer set over a bowl. Discard the contents of the strainer. Stir the confectioners' sugar into the raspberry purée. Cover the bowl with plastic wrap and let chill in the refrigerator until required.

3 Preheat the barbecue. Drain the peach halves, reserving the marinade. Cook over hot coals, turning and brushing frequently with the reserved marinade, for 3–5 minutes. To serve, put 2 scoops of vanilla ice cream in each of 4 sundae glasses, top with a peach half, and spoon the raspberry sauce over it. Decorate with whole raspberries and serve.

exotic fruity packets

SERVES	PREP	+30	COOK
4	**20** mins	**mins** marinating	**20** mins

Delicious pieces of exotic fruit are warmed through in a deliciously scented sauce to make a fabulous barbecue dessert

1 Cut the papaya in half, scoop out the seeds with a spoon, and then discard the seeds. Peel the papaya and cut the flesh into thick slices.

2 Prepare the mango by cutting it lengthwise neatly either side of the central pit.

3 Score each mango half in a criss-cross pattern. Push each mango half inside out to separate the cubes and cut them away from the peel.

4 Using a sharp knife, thickly slice the star fruit. Place all of the fruit in a bowl and mix them together.

5 Mix the grenadine and orange juice together and pour over the fruit. Marinate for at least 30 minutes.

6 Divide the fruit among 4 double-thickness squares of foil and gather up the edges to form a packet that encloses the fruit.

7 Place the foil packet on a rack set over warm coals and barbecue the fruit for 15–20 minutes.

8 Serve the fruit in the packet, with light cream or yogurt on the side.

ingredients

1 papaya
1 mango
1 star fruit
1 tbsp grenadine
3 tbsp orange juice

to serve
light cream or unsweetened
yogurt

chocolate rum bananas

SERVES **4** PREP **5** mins COOK **10** mins

Bananas are very sweet when barbecued, and conveniently come in their own protective wrapping.

1 Take four 10-inch/25-cm squares of aluminum foil and brush them with butter.

2 Cut the chocolate into very small pieces. Make a careful slit lengthwise in the peel of each banana, and open just wide enough to insert the chocolate. Place the chocolate pieces inside the bananas, along their lengths, then close them up.

3 Wrap each stuffed banana in a square of foil, then barbecue them over hot coals for about 5–10 minutes, or until the chocolate has melted inside the bananas. Remove from the barbecue, place the bananas on individual serving plates, and pour some rum into each banana.

4 Serve at once with sour cream, mascarpone cheese, or ice cream, topped with nutmeg.

ingredients

caramelized fruit medley

SERVES	PREP		COOK
4	**10** mins	**+2hrs** marinating	**8** mins

Grilling fruit brings out its full flavor and makes it simply irresistible on a summer's evening.

1 Cut the pineapple into thick slices across. Cut off the peel with a small sharp knife, then, holding each slice upright, cut out the "eyes." Stamp out the core from each slice with an apple corer. Halve the melon and scoop out the seeds with a teaspoon. Cut into thick wedges and peel with a sharp knife.

2 Mix the sherry and sugar together in a large dish, stirring until the sugar has dissolved. Add all the fruit and toss well to coat. Cover and let marinate in a cool place for 2 hours.

3 Drain the fruit, reserving the marinade. Grill the pineapple on a hot barbecue for 4 minutes, then turn over and brush with the marinade. Add the melon and grill for 2 minutes, then turn over and brush with the marinade. Add the strawberries and grill for 2 minutes. By this time, the fruit should all be golden and juicy. Serve at once.

ingredients

1 fresh pineapple
1 ogen melon
$2/3$ cup sweet sherry
generous $1/2$ cup superfine sugar
$1^1/2$ cups large strawberries

dipsmarinadescrispysaladgarlicbreadsharing
temptingaccompaniments...

sides,
sauces &
salads

crispy potato skins

SERVES
4-6

PREP
10
mins

COOK
1hr 20
mins

Use the potato flesh in this recipe for another meal, so make slightly more than you think you need.

1 Preheat the oven to 400°F/200°C. Prick the potatoes with a fork and bake in the oven for 1 hour, or until tender. Alternatively, cook in a microwave on High for 12–15 minutes. Cut the potatoes in half and scoop out the flesh, leaving about 1/4 inch/5 mm potato flesh lining the skin.

2 Preheat the barbecue. Brush the insides of the potatoes with melted butter.

3 Place the skins, cut-side down, over medium hot coals and cook for 10–15 minutes. Turn the potato skins over and cook for an additional 5 minutes, or until they are crispy. Take care that they do not burn. Season the potato skins with salt and pepper to taste and serve while they are still warm.

4 If wished, the skins can be filled with a variety of toppings. Grill the potato skins as above for 10 minutes, then turn cut-side up and sprinkle with slices of scallion, grated cheese, and chopped salami. Cook for an additional 5 minutes, or until the cheese begins to melt. Serve hot.

ingredients

8 small baking potatoes, scrubbed
1 3/4 oz/50 g butter, melted
salt and pepper

optional topping
6 scallions, sliced
1/2 cup grated Gruyère cheese
1 3/4 oz/50 g salami, cut into thin strips

garlic bread

SERVES	PREP	COOK
6	**10** mins	**15** mins

A perennial favorite, garlic bread is perfect with a range of grill meals.

ingredients

5¹/₂ oz/150 g butter, softened
3 cloves garlic, crushed
2 tbsp chopped, fresh parsley
pepper
1 large or 2 small sticks of
   French bread

1 Mix together the butter, garlic and parsley in a bowl until well combined. Season with pepper to taste and mix well.

2 Cut the French bread into thick slices.

3 Spread the flavoured butter over one side of each slice and reassemble the loaf on a large sheet of thick kitchen foil.

4 Wrap the bread well and grill over hot coals for 10–15 minutes until the butter melts and the bread is piping hot.

5 Serve as an accompaniment to a wide range of dishes.

oven home-fries

SERVES	PREP	COOK
4	10 mins	40-45 mins

The perfect barbecue accompaniment, you are sure to be popular with these tasty home-fries.

1 Preheat the oven to 400°F/200°C.

2 Cut the potatoes into thick, even-sized sticks. Rinse them under cold running water and then dry well on a clean dish towel. Put in a bowl, add the oil, and toss together until coated.

3 Spread the fries on a cookie sheet and cook in the oven for 40–45 minutes, turning once, until golden. Add salt and pepper to taste, and serve hot.

ingredients

1 lb/450 g potatoes, peeled
2 tbsp sunflower oil
salt and pepper

potato fans

SERVES	PREP	COOK
6	5 mins	1 hr

These garlic-flavored potatoes are baked in foil on the grill. They need plenty of time to cook.

1 Make a series of cuts across the potatoes almost all the way through. Cut out 6 squares of foil, each large enough to enclose a potato.

2 Place a potato on each square of foil and brush generously with the garlic flavored oil. Fold up the sides to enclose the potatoes entirely.

3 Cook over hot coals, turning occasionally, for 1 hour. To serve, open the foil parcels and gently pinch the potatoes to open up the fans.

ingredients

6 large potatoes, scrubbed but
  not peeled
2 tbsp garlic-flavored olive oil

bell pepper salad

SERVES	PREP	COOK
4	5-10 mins	35 mins

Colorful marinated Mediterranean vegetables make a tasty appetizer, especially when served with fresh bread or Tomato Toasts.

1 Cut the onion into wedges. Core and seed the bell peppers and cut into thick slices.

2 Heat the oil in a heavy-bottom skillet. Add the onion, bell peppers, zucchinis, and garlic and cook gently for 20 minutes, stirring occasionally.

3 Add the vinegar, anchovies, olives, and seasoning to taste, mix thoroughly and let cool. Spoon the cooled mixture onto individual plates and sprinkle with the basil.

4 To make the Tomato Toasts, preheat the oven to 425°F/220°C. Cut the French bread diagonally into 1/2-inch/1-cm slices. Mix the garlic, tomato, oil, and seasoning together, and spread thinly over each slice of bread.

5 Place the bread on a cookie sheet and bake in the preheated oven for 5–10 minutes, until crisp. Serve with the vegetable salad.

ingredients

1 onion
2 red bell peppers
2 yellow bell peppers
3 tbsp olive oil
2 large zucchinis, sliced
2 garlic cloves, sliced
1 tbsp balsamic vinegar
$1^3/4$ oz/50 g anchovy fillets, chopped
2 tbsp black olives, halved and pitted
salt and pepper
1 tbsp chopped fresh basil

tomato toasts
small stick of French bread
1 garlic clove, crushed
1 tomato, peeled and chopped
2 tbsp olive oil
salt and pepper

209

pasta salad with basil vinaigrette

SERVES	PREP	COOK
4	20 mins	12-15 mins

All the ingredients of pesto sauce are included in this salad, which has a fabulous summery taste, perfect for alfresco eating.

1 Cook the pasta in a large pan of lightly salted boiling water for 10–12 minutes, or until just tender but still firm to the bite. Drain the pasta, rinse under cold running water, then drain again thoroughly. Place the pasta in a large bowl.

2 Preheat the broiler to medium. To make the vinaigrette, place the basil leaves, garlic, cheese, olive oil, and lemon juice in a food processor. Season to taste with salt and pepper and process until the leaves are well chopped and the ingredients are combined. Alternatively, finely chop the basil leaves by hand and combine with the other vinaigrette ingredients. Pour the vinaigrette over the pasta and toss to coat.

3 Cut the tomatoes into wedges. Pit and halve the olives. Slice the sun-dried tomatoes. Toast the pine nuts on a cookie sheet under the hot broiler until golden.

4 Add the tomatoes (fresh and sun-dried) and the olives to the pasta and mix until combined.

5 Transfer the pasta to a serving dish, sprinkle over the Parmesan and toasted pine nuts and serve garnished with a few basil leaves.

ingredients

8 oz/225 g dried fusilli
salt and pepper
4 tomatoes
scant $^{1}/_{3}$ cup black olives
1 oz/25 g sun-dried tomatoes in oil
2 tbsp pine nuts
2 tbsp freshly grated Parmesan
  cheese

to garnish
fresh basil leaves

vinaigrette
$^{1}/_{2}$ oz/15 g basil leaves
1 garlic clove, crushed
2 tbsp freshly grated Parmesan
  cheese
4 tbsp extra-virgin olive oil
2 tbsp lemon juice

moroccan spiced salad

ingredients

2 tbsp olive oil
scant $^1/_2$ cup long-grain rice
$1^3/_4$ cups water
4 tbsp lemon-flavored or
  extra-virgin olive oil
3 tbsp vinegar
1 tbsp lemon juice
1 tbsp honey
1 tsp garam masala
1 tsp ground coriander
$^1/_2$ tsp mustard
8 oz/225 g canned red kidney beans
8 oz/225 g canned garbanzos
2 shallots, chopped
4 scallions, trimmed and sliced
$2^1/_4$ oz/60 g pine nuts
$3^1/_2$ oz/100 g golden raisins
1 tbsp chopped fresh mint

to garnish
chopped fresh mint

to serve
wedges of fresh lemon

SERVES	PREP	COOK
4	15 mins	40 mins

This superb salad is great for vegetarians and non-vegetarians alike, full of flavor, texture and healthy foods.

1 Heat the olive oil in a large pan. Add the rice and cook for 3 minutes, stirring, over low heat. Pour in the water and bring to a boil, then lower the heat, cover, and simmer for 35 minutes. Remove from the heat and transfer to a strainer. Rinse under cold running water, drain well, and set aside to cool.

2 In a large bowl, mix together the lemon-flavored or extra-virgin olive oil, vinegar, lemon juice, and honey. Add the garam masala, coriander, and mustard and stir well.

3 Add the rice and mix well. Rinse and drain the kidney beans and garbanzos, then add them to the bowl with the shallots, scallions, pine nuts, golden raisins, and mint. Divide between serving bowls, garnish with chopped fresh mint, and serve with lemon wedges.

avocado salad with lime dressing

SERVES	PREP	COOK
4	20 mins	0 mins

ingredients

2¹/4 oz/60 g mixed fresh red
  and green lettuce leaves
21/4 oz/60 g fresh arugula
4 scallions, finely diced
5 tomatoes, sliced
¹/4 cup chopped walnuts,
  toasted
2 avocados
1 tbsp lemon juice

lime dressing
1 tbsp lime juice
1 tsp Dijon mustard
1 tbsp crème fraîche or sour
  cream
1 tbsp chopped fresh parsley
  or cilantro
3 tbsp extra-virgin olive oil
pinch of sugar
salt and pepper

This salad must be served fresh to prevent discolouration and floppy salad leaves.

1 Wash and drain the lettuce and arugula, if necessary. Shred all the leaves and arrange in the bottom of a large salad bowl. Add the scallions, tomatoes, and walnuts.

2 Halve, peel, and pit the avocados and cut into thin slices or small chunks. Brush with the lemon juice to prevent discoloration, then transfer to the salad bowl. Mix together gently.

3 Put the dressing ingredients into a screw-top jar, screw on the lid tightly, and shake well until thoroughly combined. Drizzle the dressing over the salad and serve immediately.

salade niçoise

SERVES	PREP	COOK
4	12-15 mins	13-17 mins

This Provençal dish is probably the best-known and best-loved classic salad in the Western world.

1 Cook the eggs, potatoes, and beans simultaneously. Place the eggs in a pan and cover with cold water. Bring to a boil, then reduce the heat and boil gently for 12 minutes. Cook the potatoes in a pan of lightly salted boiling water for 12–15 minutes, or until tender, and cook the green beans in a separate pan of lightly salted boiling water for 3–5 minutes.

2 Meanwhile, prepare all the remaining ingredients. Coarsely chop the lettuces, drain and flake the tuna, then drain the anchovies and halve them lengthwise. Chop the tomatoes and slice the scallions. To make the dressing, place all the ingredients in a large salad bowl and beat well to mix.

3 Drain the beans and refresh in cold water. Add to the salad bowl with the lettuces, tuna, anchovies, tomatoes, scallions, olives, and capers. Drain the eggs, cool under cold running water and set aside. Drain the potatoes and add to the salad. Lightly toast the pine nuts in a dry skillet, shaking the skillet frequently, for 1–2 minutes, or until golden. Sprinkle them over the salad. Shell and chop the eggs and add them to the salad.

4 Whisk the dressing again, add it to the salad, toss to coat, and serve.

ingredients

2 eggs
12 small new potatoes
salt
4 oz/115 g green beans
2 romaine lettuces or 3 Boston lettuces
7 oz/200 g canned tuna in oil
6 canned anchovy fillets
4 tomatoes
4 scallions
12 black olives
2 tbsp bottled capers, drained
2 tbsp pine nuts

dressing

6 tbsp extra virgin olive oil
2 tbsp tarragon vinegar
1 tsp Dijon mustard
1 garlic clove, finely chopped

sweet & sour marinade

SERVES	PREP	COOK
4	5 mins	0 mins

Sweet and sour is a classic taste combination and will always be popular.

ingredients

1 cup orange, grapefruit, or
 pineapple juice
2 tbsp sweet sherry
$^1/_2$ cup dark soy sauce
$^1/_2$ cup chicken stock
$^1/_4$ cup apple vinegar
1 tbsp tomato paste
$^1/_4$ cup light brown sugar
1 tsp powdered garlic
1 tsp ground ginger

1 Combine the fruit juice, sherry, soy sauce, chicken stock, and apple vinegar in a mixing bowl.

2 Stir in the tomato paste, sugar, garlic, and ginger. Mix well.

3 This mixture can be used to marinate and baste chicken or pork.

minted yogurt marinade

SERVES	PREP	COOK
4	**10** mins	**0** mins

ingredients

2 garlic cloves, crushed
1 tsp salt
4 tbsp finely chopped fresh mint
1 cup plain yogurt
1 tsp ground cumin, coriander
  seeds, or cinnamon, optional
1 onion (optional)

You can prepare this marinade in advance and chill in the refrigerator until needed.

1 Mix the garlic with the salt to make a smooth paste. Turn into a mixing bowl and stir in the mint, yogurt, and cumin, coriander, or cinnamon.

2 If you are using the onion, place it in a food processor, together with the yogurt mixture, and blend for a few seconds, or until the mixture is coarse and the onion is blended in.

3 Use to marinate and baste lamb.

tomato salsa

ingredients

4 ripe red tomatoes
1 medium red onion or 6 scallions
1–2 garlic cloves, crushed
  (optional)
2 tbsp chopped fresh cilantro
$1/2$ red or green chili (optional)
finely grated zest of $1/2$–1 lemon
  or lime
1–2 tbsp lemon or lime juice
pepper

SERVES	PREP	COOK
4	10 mins	0 mins

This salad is used extensively in Mexican cooking and served as a dip or a relish, and is eaten as an accompaniment to almost any dish.

1 Chop the tomatoes fairly finely and evenly, and put into a bowl. They must be firm and a good strong red color for the best results, but if preferred, they may be peeled by placing them in boiling water for about 20 seconds and then plunging into cold water. The skins should then slip off easily when they are nicked with a knife.

2 Peel and slice the red onion thinly, or trim the scallions and cut into thin slanting slices; add to the chopped tomatoes with the garlic and coriander and mix lightly.

3 Remove the seeds from the red or green chili, chop the flesh very finely, and add to the salad. Treat the chilies with care; do not touch your eyes or face after handling them until you have washed your hands thoroughly. Chili juices can burn.

4 Add the lemon or lime zest and juice to the salsa, and mix well. Transfer the salsa to a serving bowl and sprinkle with pepper.

honey mustard marinade

SERVES
4

PREP
5
mins

COOK
0
mins

This sweet tangy marinade is perfect to baste meat or vegetables.

1 Combine all the ingredients, except the oil, in a small mixing bowl.

2 Gradually add the oil, whisking constantly, until it is fully absorbed into the mixture.

3 Use to marinate and baste chicken or pork, especially spare ribs.

ingredients

2 tbsp honey
2 tbsp wholegrain mustard
1 tsp ground ginger
1 tsp garlic powder
2 tsp finely chopped fresh rosemary
4 tbsp dark soy sauce
$^1/_4$ cup olive oil

index

index